# THE POCKET BOOK OF
# ST PATRICK

Gill Books
Hume Avenue, Park West, Dublin 12

www.gillbooks.ie

Gill Books is an imprint of M.H. Gill & Co.

Copyright © Teapot Press Ltd 2026

ISBN: 978-1-8045-8485-9

This book was created and produced by Teapot Press Ltd

Written by Rachel Pierce
Designed by Tony Potter

Printed in Europe

This book is typeset in Garamond & Dax

All rights reserved.

No part of this publication may be copied, reproduced or transmitted in any form or by any means, without permission of the publishers.

To the best of our knowledge, this book complies in full with the requirements of the General Product Safety Regulation (GPSR). For further information and help with any safety queries, please contact us at productsafety@gill.ie

A CIP catalogue record for this book is available from the British Library.

5 4 3 2 1

# THE POCKET BOOK OF
# ST PATRICK
#### Life, Legend and Legacy

## Rachel Pierce

Gill Books

# Contents

6     Introduction: Patrick – The Man We Think We Know

14    Chapter 1: Patrick's World

28    Chapter 2: From Boy to Slave

46    Chapter 3: Freedom and Faith

66    Chapter 4: Patrick the Missionary

88    Chapter 5: Patrick at the End of his Life

106   Chapter 6: The Patrick of Legend

140   Chapter 7: Holy Traditions and Sacred Relics

160   Chapter 8: St Patrick in Art

176   Chapter 9: In Patrick's Footsteps – The Pilgrim Paths

| | |
|---|---|
| 196 | Chapter 10: Visiting Patrick's Ireland |
| 222 | Chapter 11: The Greening of the Irish – St Patrick's Day in Ireland |
| 238 | Chapter 12: The Greening of the World – St Patrick's Day Beyond Ireland |
| 252 | Epilogue: Legacy of a Holy Man |
| 256 | Picture Credits |

*Be always ours this day and for evermore.*
*Christ beside me,*
*Christ before me,*
*Christ behind me,*
*Christ within me,*
*Christ beneath me,*
*Christ above me.*
*If I have any worth, it is to live my life for God.*

## INTRODUCTION:
# Patrick – The Man We Think We Know

*Notwithstanding that I am in many things imperfect I want my brethren and kinsmen to know what sort of man I am.*

From *Confession*

Statue of St Patrick, Croagh Patrick, County Mayo. The pilgrimage route to the summit of Croagh Patrick begins at the statue of the saint.

It seems safe to assume that when people hear the words 'St Patrick', the first thought to come to mind is snakes. The most enduring and dearly held belief about the saint is that he rid Ireland of serpents, casting them out in the name of God. It is a legend that, along with all the other legends that have long since grown around him, has obscured a truly fascinating episode in history. While St Patrick, the patron saint of Ireland, is known and celebrated worldwide, what is known is not the whole story, and often not the true story, of Patricius, an extraordinary man who transformed a country within his lifetime.

The legends are colourful and fantastical and make for great storytelling, but the true story of Patrick, the boy who became a slave who became a saint, is both compelling and deeply moving. There are no proven dates for Patrick, but it is largely accepted that he was born in Roman Britain *c.*385–392. At the age of sixteen he was stolen away by a raiding party and brought to Ireland, where he was sold into slave labour. For six years he lived as a shepherd, out on the cold, rain-lashed hills, sleeping in mean huts, no doubt hungry and exhausted. He was assailed by homesickness and loneliness. He was in a strange land, where the people spoke a strange language, and yet he was the stranger, the foreigner, the slave.

After six years, Patrick managed to escape. To date, he is the only Roman citizen known to have escaped from slavery. He returned to his family, the prodigal son, but the faith that he had discovered during those six terrible years, that had sustained him throughout, now burned in him like a fire, obliterating all thoughts of a comfortable life lived out at home. His heart belonged to God, and that led him to study to become a priest, and then be ordained a bishop. During this time he suffered a trial by his peers based on an allegation made by a friend of his – a man he trusted and who betrayed him. That experience was one of the most difficult of Patrick's life, but he put his faith in God's understanding and forgiveness and he overcame that deep betrayal of trust.

Now a missionary, Patrick returned to Ireland *c.*432, to find an island and people that had not changed in the two decades he was away. Once again he arrived on a small boat, but this time he came as God's ambassador, a preacher with a crystal-clear goal from which he would not be diverted: to convert the people of Ireland to a belief in Christ the Saviour. His mission was one of the most successful ever witnessed in history. It is true that other Christian missionaries had spread the word in Ireland before him, but Patrick travelled and spoke tirelessly, engaging the people, persuading them, showing them God's love through his own actions, converting them in their thousands. It has often been described as a 'bloodless battle' because it stood in marked contrast to the religious battles across Europe, as Christianity fought to become the dominant religion. In Ireland, there was no blood spilled. This in itself seems a minor miracle, but we can only surmise that Patrick's approach, manner of speaking, deep-seated belief and ability to speak Irish, learned as a slave, all combined to make him a convincing and persuasive voice for his God. The people believed him and chose to follow him.

Patrick never returned home again. It pained him greatly to live in exile – *'I would most dearly love to … see my homeland and family'* – but he stuck fast to his goal and lived among the Irish people for the rest of his life. He died on 17 March *c.*461, a man with about 70 winters on his head, humble and fiercely committed until the end of his days. His was a life shaped by adversity, which led him to seek a deeper purpose, and in that mission he built a legacy that extended through all the centuries that followed, right up to the present day. That is an extraordinary achievement: Patrick heralded a new Ireland, leading the whole island away from paganism and the rule of the druids towards a belief in God that would form the most dominant religion by far until the twentieth century.

He shaped a nation and in bringing Christianity – with its schools of learning, its monk scribes, its illuminated manuscripts and its important artworks – he also contributed hugely to how Ireland became the land of saints and scholars. His story is intimately bound up with Ireland's history.

What is truly incredible is that we know any of this story at all. Patrick lived in the fifth century, over 1,500 years ago. Historians have precious little first-hand evidence about the people who lived in Ireland and Britain at that time, so our knowledge of Patrick stands as something unique. The reason for this is that two documents written by Patrick's own hand have survived, recorded within the ninth-century Book of Armagh. One is a letter, written by Patrick, as bishop, to admonish the chieftain Coroticus and his men for seizing and enslaving a group of new converts. This is Patrick at his work, setting out God's law, urging moral behaviour, threatening excommunication for those who went against God's will.

The other document is the *Confession,* dictated when Patrick was an old man, looking back on his life. This is the only autobiographical text remaining from that period. It provides a remarkable insight into Patrick as man and as holy man. Cardinal Tomás Ó Fiaich noted the huge importance of this document: *'Since the historian depends mainly on written documents for his knowledge of the past, Irish history properly speaking must begin with St Patrick, the author of the earliest documents known to have been written in Ireland.'* So alongside his Christian legacy, Patrick also brought the language of Latin and literature to Ireland, giving us our earliest writing on historical record.

The quote opposite is from the *Confession* and it gives us Patrick's own stated desire: *'I want my brethren and kinsmen to know what sort of man I am'*. In the medieval period, writers embellished Patrick's story, turning him into the hero of legend, conflating the real and the fantastical to make him seem almost superhuman. That layer of storytelling has lain over the story of Patrick ever since, like a culvert over a river. Our purpose here is to uncover the true story of Patricius/Patrick, to find out what sort of man he was, to follow the history, to read his own words, and to hear his voice as it speaks to us across the centuries.

*'I want my brethren and kinsmen to know what sort of man I am.'*

## Myth vs fact

✤ There is a general view that St Patrick is as Irish as Irish can be, so it often comes as a shock when people realise he wasn't Irish at all – and that the patron saint of Ireland is, in fact, a British man.

## CHAPTER 1:
# Patrick's World

*I am Patrick, a sinner, unlettered ... I am the son of Calpornius, a deacon, son of Potitus, a priest. My father lived at the village of Bannavem Taburniae, for he had an estate nearby, where I was taken captive at about sixteen years old.*

From *Confession*

Patrick is captured by Irish raiders, *The Illustrated London News*, 1900 (colourised).

The world into which Patrick was born was in a state of dangerous flux. When he was born at the end of the fourth century (*c.*385–392), Britain had been part of the Roman empire for over three centuries, but its power was starting to wane and its stability was coming under increasing pressure. The Romans had built a massive empire: from its northern frontier on the island of Britain, it stretched 5,000km right across to Arabia in southwest Asia. But as new enemies rose up to challenge Roman rule, such as the marauding Goths, those borders became more and more difficult to hold firm.

Patrick would have been born Patricius, given that he was a Roman citizen. In the *Confession* he tells us that his father *'lived at the village of Bannavem Taburniae, for he had an estate nearby'*. There has been, and continues to be, much speculation as to the location of his home place. There are competing theories – some argue for North Wales, some for Lancashire – but chief among them is the suggestion that Bannavem was in the county of Cumbria, perhaps in or around present-day Carlisle. This location is close to the coast, which allows for the seaborne raiders who kidnapped him. It is also close to the Lake District, lying about 70km distant, where the placename Patterdale suggests an origin in 'Patrick's well'. Wherever its exact location, the name implies that it was a Celtic-British district, which means Patrick probably spoke a local Celtic language alongside being educated through Latin.

The *'estate'* he describes was likely a Roman villa with a farm. His was a comfortable existence, in a relatively well-off family attended by servants. His grandfather, Potitus, was a priest *(presbyter)*, although the young Patrick did not feel any call to follow in his footsteps, describing himself as having *'an unbelieving*

The Dovedale and Patterdale valleys in England, possible location for St Patrick's birthplace.

*mind'*. His father, Calpornius, was a decurion *(decurio)* – a local official who was appointed to help with tax collection and the administration of civil matters. Calpornius was also a deacon in the Church, which no doubt brought with it a high level of standing in the local community. So the young Patrick would have been used to being part of a well-regarded, respectable and relatively wealthy landowning family. If his own testimony is to be believed, this life of comfort and ease spoiled him, causing him to languish in his *'unbelieving'*, safe in his *'youth and ignorance'*, with no fear for any consequences this might bring. To the cosseted young man, his future must have seemed pre-mapped and dependable, backed by family wealth and security. Surely it was all written in the stars?

The Romans had brought their modern infrastructure and innovations to Britain. The times in which Patrick's parents and grandparents grew up would have seen the proliferation of the famed Roman roads, those great feats of engineering. They built *c.*16,000km of roads throughout Britain, connecting towns and cities, and opening up the country and the economy with these reliable travel and trade routes. They also transformed the look of those cities and towns and villages with their architecture and aesthetic sense. The Celtic hill forts of the past were slowly abandoned as the Roman way of life became the norm. The cities were adorned with theatres, baths, villas and public sculptures, the beautiful architecture for which Rome was renowned. The villas of the wealthy featured mosaic floors and some even had underfloor heating. The archaeological remains of the Roman era in Britain show that the aesthetic culture was suffused through all aspects of life.

As part of the safeguarding of this proud civilising force, Roman garrisons manned the borders of the empire, keeping their citizens within their jurisdiction and keeping all foreign 'barbarians' out. The northernmost frontier was marked by Hadrian's Wall, which runs for *c.*118km, from Wallsend in the east to the Solway Firth on the west coast, and in places bisects the county of Cumbria. This was a fortified barrier, designed to keep

A three-dimensional render of a typical Roman villa.

the wild northerners beyond the border and prevent an incursion from that quarter. Today, the wall divides present-day England and Scotland. Along its length were manned towers and milecastles, which were small forts with a gate allowing access through the

wall to those approved for entry or exit by the Roman soldiers. In this way, the cross-border movement of people, goods and animals could be monitored and, when deemed necessary, prevented.

There was, however, another source of threat that was more

Hadrian's Wall.

Milecastle 39 on Hadrian's Wall.

*'The uttermost part of the earth'*

difficult to control and defend. About 295km away across the Irish Sea lay an island that had never been subjected to Roman rule. The maps of old sometimes warned, *'Here be dragons'* – and it is easy to imagine that those looking across the water towards Hibernia felt it might be one such place. Iron Age Ireland was occupied by a Celtic people, who were led by the wisdom of the druids, entertained by the stories of the bards, and governed by chiefs who presided over their small 'kingdoms'. There was no Latin spoken there, no straight, hard roads connecting and mapping the land, no grand houses – and certainly no underfloor heating. It was seen as a heathen place, un-Christianised, un-Romanised and frankly undesirable. Who would be foolish enough to leave Britain and its well ordered social hierarchy to visit an island that appeared to relish living in the savage past?

It is true that merchants plied their trade

across the water between the two islands, so no doubt there was cross-pollination of ideas and cultural mores, and it is likely the Irish Celts were well aware of the Christian religion, but the difference between the two remained stark. Celtic Ireland was an outpost, the last point west for travellers from Europe, after which the rough and wide Atlantic took over and no land could be seen on the horizon. Patrick described it as *'the uttermost part of the earth'* – an outlier that marked the boundary of civilisation. As far as Roman Britain was concerned, its neighbouring island was a lawless backwater, and while trade could be beneficial, these barbarians had to be kept at bay, just the same as those wild ones living north of Hadrian's Wall.

As is ever the case in the history of human society, changing political circumstances and loyalties undermined the empire and sowed the seeds of its demise.

## Did you know?

✤ The world calls him Patrick, but St Patrick's true name was Patricius. His *Confession,* a declaration of his life written by his own hand, begins with the words: *Ego Patricius* (I am Patrick).

The departure of the Roman legions - a traditional view. From Cassell's *History of England,* 1909 edition.

While Patrick was enjoying his happy rural childhood, the winds of change were blowing hard across the empire, eventually making themselves felt at its western edge in Britain. The fall of the empire is dated to around 409, but it was in effect a long, slow decline over many years. However, one of the first major consequences at this time, when Patrick was a teenaged boy, was the loss of the Roman legions in many parts of Britain. This left the borders unprotected, providing lucrative opportunities for the raiders who had previously been held at bay. There were threats to life and livelihood from land and sea. It was only a matter of time before the 'barbarians' burst their way through and invaded with intent.

In the *Confession,* Patrick tells us that he was kidnapped at the age of sixteen, but he doesn't describe the raiders coming and the terror they must have brought with them. Therefore, we can only imagine how traumatising the ordeal was for his village and his family. The raiders were Irish pirates, crossing the sea in search of slave labour, which would fetch a good price back home in Ireland. We must imagine they were armed, fierce, descending on the household in a frenzy of shouts and roars, rounding up the household, then roughly tying them to prevent escape, before taking the captured ones to the waiting ships. They must have been sick with fear and dread, knowing that wherever they ended up, it would be far, far worse than where they were leaving. Their liberty was gone – how long would they hold onto their lives?

Patrick describes in the *Confession* how the raiders *'took me captive and carried off the menservants and maidservants of my father's house'*. It seems that he was not separated, as the young master of the villa, but was lumped in with all the other unfortunates the pirates had seized. From now on, Patrick was just another slave, just another body to exploit, just another back to break with hard graft. In this new state of affairs he was no different from his servants, and no fine clothes or social status could save him from the same fate as everyone else.

The question of what that fate would be must have gnawed at him as he was put into the boat that would take him away from all he had ever known. Would he ever see his family again? His home?

## Did you know?

✤ Patrick was kidnapped by Irish pirates and spirited away across the sea to Ireland. This crossing would have been made in home-made boats, akin to currachs or coracles. Patrick would have sailed in a boat made of a wooden frame, with animal hides covering it, held in place by leather thongs. It is no wonder the oceans and seas were as frightening as they were compelling, given journeys had to be made in such vulnerable vessels.

A medieval manuscript showing St Brendan in the kind of vessel that brought Patrick to Ireland.

Coracle fishers in the early twentieth century.

Or would he die in a foreign land? And what had he heard tell of the land across the water to where the pirates were now transporting him? The word 'barbarians' was often used to describe the pagans who lived on that island, so Patrick must have felt deep anxiety as to what was awaiting him there.

In time to come, he would look on this terrifying snatching into captivity as a judgement and punishment from God:

> *I did not know the true God, and for this reason I was led in captivity to Ireland, with so many thousands of people. It was in accordance with our deserts, because we had forsaken God and did not keep His commandments, and were not obedient to our bishops who used to admonish us for our salvation. God brought to bear upon us the wrath of His anger and scattered us among many peoples, even to the uttermost part of the earth.*

If it was a punishment from his God, it was a severe one. Patrick was brutally ripped from his home, his people, his life; shorn of everything that made him who he was; cast into an indifferent world where he would be the lowest of the low: a slave. He was leaving a boy: would he ever return? Patrick could never have dreamed it then, but this life-shattering experience was in fact the first step on his path to God, to sainthood, and to his own far-reaching legacy.

## CHAPTER 2:
# From Boy to Slave

*I dwell among strangers*

From *Confession*

A painting of St Patrick by Jacob Popcak.

The Irish raiding party crossed the sea with its plunder – the boy Patrick among the many who had been stolen away. Their final destination was the island sometimes referred to as *ultima Thule* – a Latin term to describe the furthest place on Earth, the last edge of the known world, the end of civilisation. There has been much speculation as to where the boats may have landed on Ireland's coast. Did they cross the narrow North Channel and land on the northeastern coast? And if they did so, was it far north – perhaps around modern-day Belfast – or was it down along the eastern coast near Drogheda and the mouth of the River Boyne, then known as Inber Colpa? Wherever their docking and disembarking point, once back on dry land Patrick was herded into Iron Age Ireland, still a Celtic stronghold, and into his life as one of the unfree, a slave to be bought and sold.

Sixteenth-century Maiden Tower, among the sand dunes at the mouth of the River Boyne.

Patrick doesn't describe the crossing or the landing or his captors, but that hasn't prevented colourful tales entwining themselves around his journey. There is a long-told tale that says his captor was Niall of the Nine Hostages (Niall Noígíallach), a legendary 'high king' of Ireland. This dramatic embellishment seems to date to Geoffrey Keating's *Foras Feasa ar Éirinn (History of Ireland)*, which Keating, a priest and historian, completed around 1634. That story grew its own new details, and right into the twentieth-century Irish schoolchildren were taught that Patrick was transported to the Hill of Tara, where Niall Noígíallach imprisoned him and some of his fellow slaves in the Mound of the Hostages. The Hill of Tara holds an extremely important place in the Celtic history of Ireland, said to be where the palace of the high king of Ireland stood and from where he reigned, and the grass-covered remains of a major hilltop complex can still be seen there. It is considered a sacred place, the location of the Lia Fáil, or stone of destiny. This upright stone was said to cry out when the true High King stood or sat on it, becoming his coronation stone. Near the Lia Fáil lies the Mound of the Hostages, a cold, hard stone 'cave' with a bare, muddy floor. If the young Patrick was held there, it would have been a grim and bleak place to lodge. But there is nothing to corroborate this story as being part of his experience of arriving in Hibernia.

## The land of the Celts

What is known, according to Patrick's own testimony in the *Confession,* is that he was bought by a farmer and taken to work as a herdsman. The familiar story is that Patrick was brought to Slemish, in County Antrim, and that was his station for the six years of his life as a slave. To this day, Slemish is a site of pilgrimage for those wishing to follow in the footsteps of Patrick. However, it is not mentioned in the *Confession.* There is only one placename given by Patrick himself, when he refers to *'the wood of Voclut, which is near the Western sea'.* This has been interpreted as referring to Foclut in County Mayo. Archaeologist and historian Liam de Paor concluded that *'The weight of the evidence is that this was a wood in the West of Ireland, in what is now County Mayo, on the western shore of Killala Bay'.* If that is the case, the slave Patrick would have travelled over 200km to reach his new 'home'.

On his travels from east coast to west coast, Patrick would have had his first sight of this fabled island and its fearsome Celts, described by ancient Greek historian Diodorus Siculus (first century BC) as *'terrifying in appearance … boasters and threateners and given to bombastic self dramatization'.* At that time, the population was very small, only around 250,000 people. They depended on rearing cattle and sheep, as well as some arable farming. Ireland was an island of forests then, broken up by wide plains, bogland and marsh. There were wild animals roaming the countryside, such as boars and wolves. There were wild geese, cranes and golden eagles flying overhead; wild swans gracing the many rivers and lakes.

Celtic Ireland didn't have towns and villages like Patrick's own island; instead it still had the tribal system of *tuatha*, which comprised about 150 small 'kingdoms' presided over by a chief or king. Each isolated *tuath* was a farmstead within and around a ring fort. The circular fort was surrounded and protected by an earthen bank or by a ditch and stone wall. The animals could be brought within the fort for safekeeping.

A farmstead.

The social structure within the tuath was headed by the chief and his family, then the nobles, the freemen and finally the slaves, as Patrick now was. The chief was the ruler in times of peace and the leading warrior in times of war. The nobles often counted druids, poets and sometimes craftsmen among their number – all roles that were revered by the people. The laws of the land were the ancient Brehon laws, preserved and enforced by judges. The druids were the trusted advisors of the chief, well versed in magic and divination, leading Patrick to describe the Irish as *'they who never had knowledge of God, but up until now always worshipped only idols and abominations'.* To Patrick, this anachronistic culture, based on ancient ways, must have felt like a strange sort of time travel – he had left an innovative, ambitious, forward-looking Roman Britain and now was living in a society that would have been familiar mainly from his history lessons.

Perhaps, as they made their way west, Patrick saw tall standing stones etched with lines and ridges. These were the only form of writing in Ireland at that time – ogham writing. Ogham is thought to date to *c.*AD300 and was called after Ogmios, the Celtic god of writing. The lines represented letters of the archaic Irish alphabet and were carved onto standing stones, which are thought to have served as gravestones and boundary markers. Irish

Carving of Ogham letters into a stone pillar.

was the language of the stones and of the people – a language that would have rendered Patrick mute, his Latin useless for conversing.

We can only wonder at what he was thinking and feeling as he was conveyed across this alien country. He was a mere strip of a lad, sixteen years old, and here he was, profoundly alone, no doubt frightened and anxious, with no way of knowing what lay ahead or how long his ordeal would last. Did he feel defeated, or did he vow to survive?

When Patrick reached the farmer's lands, he was sent out into the wilds to tend the sheep and guard them against attack. This would have been hard labour, out on the hills in all weathers, invaded by the perishing cold, suffering the pitch-dark of night, listening for the cries of wolves or other predators, tensed for attack, homesick to his very bones. This was to be his life for the next six years. He must have had a sense of being taken out of himself, almost unrecognisable to himself, having to embrace this new identity that was forced upon him: *'I have had to change my language and speak that of a foreign people.'*

## The power of prayer

In his loneliness and loss, Patrick found himself praying to God for solace. Throughout his period of slavery in Ireland, this is what sustained him. He discovered that although robbed of everyone he had ever loved or known, he carried within him an intimate friend, a confidant, an ever-listening ear: his God. He saw himself as living until now as an unbeliever, for which he was roundly punished with this abduction into slavery. But now, through prayer, he comes to understand that *'the Lord ... looked upon my abjection, and had mercy on my youth and ignorance, and watched over me before I knew Him, and before I came to be wise, or to discern between good and evil; and He kept me safe and comforted me as a father would his son'*.

Patrick began to pray day and night, reciting the comforting words over and over again, like a mantra against his surreal new reality. He asked God to protect him, to stay with him, and as he said these prayers and felt their effect on him, he grew in devotion and in certainty that he was indeed protected and cherished by the Lord. His own words in the *Confession* powerfully describe this:

*But after I came to Ireland I was daily herding flocks – I used to pray many times a day – more and more the love of God and the fear of Him came to me, and my faith was increased, and my spirit was moved so that in one day I would pray as many as a hundred times, and in the night nearly as often, even while I was staying in the woods and on the mountains; and before daylight I used to be stirred to prayer, in snow, in frost, in rain; and I felt no ill effects from it, nor was there any sluggishness in me, such as now I see there is, because then the spirit was fervent in me.*

This seemingly unlikely revelation of his relationship with God would shape Patrick's whole life. For now, on windswept Irish hills, he knew only that prayer gave him a bulwark against despair, but it was affecting him in ways that would change him forever. He was punished, but at the same time he was being forgiven. This was his penance, and he threw himself into it wholeheartedly.

Centuries later, the medieval author of the *Tripartite Life* would compose a poem said to be based on the words Patrick repeated over and over during this time. While not written by Patrick himself, these words have come to be firmly associated with him and seem to reverberate with the spiritual devotion of the slave Patrick. This is the much-loved Lorica, or St Patrick's Breastplate, or The Deer's Cry, a beautiful and heartfelt prayer for protection:

*Christ by, Christ before me,*
    *Christ behind me,*
*Christ within me, Christ beneath me,*
    *Christ above me,*
*Christ on my left hand,*
    *Christ on my right,*
*Christ in the breast of all who behold me*
*Christ on the tongues of all who talk of me*
*Christ in every eye that sees me*
*Christ in every ear that hears me.*
(trans. Thomas Kinsella, 1957)

So now emerges the shadow of the saint to come. Patrick is a slave in a foreign land, but he is also transformed by that

## Escape!

One night, he dreams of a voice speaking directly to him: '*… you who are soon to go to your own country*'. The voice goes quiet then, but '*after a little while again I heard a voice say to me: "Look, your ship is ready".*' That imperative to *Look* suggests Patrick was shown a vision of the future, of where he needed to go. There must have been some intimation of what this ship and this place would look like because he tells us that '*It was not nearby, but was at a distance of perhaps two hundred miles; and I had never been there, nor did I know anybody there.*' So it cannot have been the place where he landed as a slave six years before. Patrick has been shown an unknown port, and a waiting ship. This is his chance to make his escape, under the watchful eye of his God who is showing him the way. He must have known the dangers that lay ahead, the punishment for a runaway slave, the slim chances of managing to cross such a distance on foot safely, but Patrick did not hesitate: '*Shortly after that I took to flight, left the man with whom I had been for six years, and journeyed by the power of God, who directed my way unto my good, and I feared nothing until I reached that ship.*'

It was just as he had been promised – when he reaches the place he was shown in his dream, a ship is lying at anchor, preparing to depart. Patrick approaches the crew, but he is warned off, told in no uncertain terms that he will not be allowed on board to travel with them. As he has done for six long years, Patrick turns to prayer, reciting the words to call upon God's mercy and protection. He hasn't even finished when he hears a shout and he is beckoned back to the ship, where they crew tell him they will *'take you on trust'*. Whatever he endured on his 200-mile trek to get here, it has been worth it. His passage has been secured, *'and straight away we set sail'*.

The sailors were 'heathens' but Patrick *'rather hoped that some of them would come to faith in Jesus Christ'*. He clearly already has the missionary's zeal and a desire to share his strong faith with others. They are three days at sea before reaching land again, although it is uncertain where they landed – it could have been the south coast of Britain, perhaps Wales or Cornwall, or on the French coast. The place they landed was an empty land and they couldn't find a scrap of food to eat. They walked for twenty-eight days, getting hungrier and more desperate. Eventually, the captain demanded to know why Patrick's great God didn't help them. Patrick saw his chance. *'I said confidently to them: "Turn sincerely with all your heart to the*

*Lord my God, because nothing is impossible to Him, so that today he may send food in your way until you are satisfied.'*

What happened next seemed a miracle: a herd of pigs came trundling their way. The men fell on them with glee, slaughtering and slashing. They could fill their bellies once again and not die on the wayside in this *'deserted country'*. *'After this,'* reports Patrick, *'they gave their full thanks to God, and I became honourable in their eyes.'* This was his first taste of being an ambassador for the Lord.

The wild pigs were roasted and eaten.

All this time Patrick was still experiencing strange dreams and visions. One was particularly vivid and terrifying: *'… I was sleeping when Satan mightily put me to the test – I shall remember it as long as I am in this body. He fell upon me like a huge rock, and I could not move a limb.'* This sleep paralysis only ended when Patrick cried out *'Helias, Helias'* – *'Sun, Sun'*. In that moment, a long shaft of sunlight fell across his body and he was freed, *'and I believe that I was aided by Christ my Lord'*.

## Prodigal son

Somewhat like the travels of Odysseus, Patrick's journey home must have been filled with adventure and sidetracks and delays. In fact, he was captured again – although he doesn't say who the captors were. But on his first night enslaved, yet again, a *'divine voice'* tells him that this will only last two months. Sure enough, *'on the sixtieth night the Lord delivered me from their hands'*. Finally, *'after a few years'*, he made his way back to Britain and to his family home. We can only imagine the welcome he received – surely his family and friends had given him up for dead by now, after seeing him carried off trussed up in ropes? There must have been a tearful reunion. His family wanted to keep him close and safe after all that he had been through: *'my family ... received me as a son, and sincerely begged of me that at least now, after all the many troubles I had endured I should not leave them to go anywhere.'* It is easy to understand his family's desire to hold onto their son, not to be parted ever again, to never again to lose him to a hostile land and hostile people. But they were to find out that God had other plans for Patrick.

## Did you know?

✤ The locations of Celtic ring forts can be traced through modern placenames. There were five terms used to describe these forts: *dún*, *rath* and *lios* referred to forts with an earthen bank around them; *cathair* and *caiseal* indicated a fort surrounded by a stone wall and ditch. These words are common in placenames all around the island to this day.

Aerial view of ancient Celtic stone ring fort remains in Ireland.

*From Boy to Slave*

## Myth vs fact

✤ We will never know if the raiding party that kidnapped the young Patrick was led by Niall of the Nine Hostages. That remains a myth, but it is tempting to believe because it would lend his story a very pleasing symmetry given that Saint Colmcille (AD521–*c*.597) was Niall's great-great-grandson. Colmcille was one of the key saints who took up the baton of Christianity and continued Patrick's work of conversion and worship.

✤ It has long been taken as a fact that Slemish, an imposing flat-topped mountain in County Antrim, was Patrick's home for the six years of his slavery in Ireland. However, it is never mentioned by Patrick in the *Confession*. It has assumed the status of fact, but for now at least it remains part of the mythical story that grew up around Patrick's time in Ireland.

Slemish Mountain at sunset.

## CHAPTER 3:
# Freedom and Faith

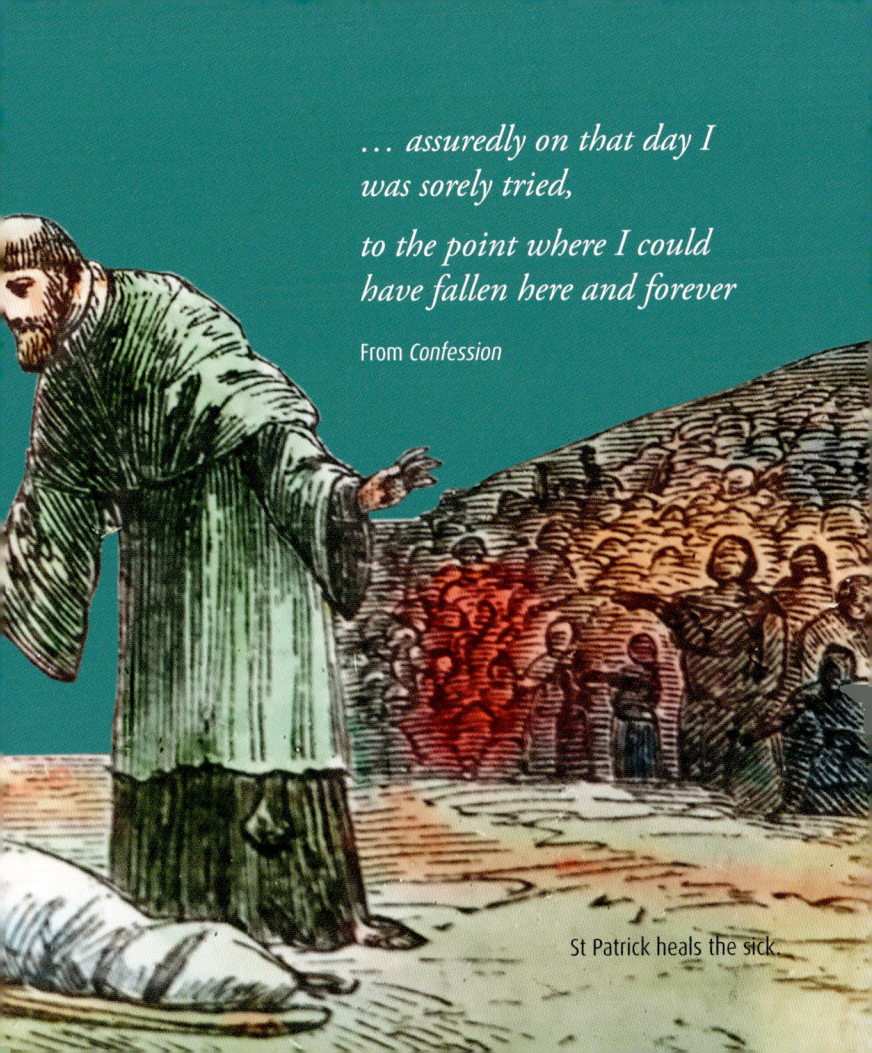

St Patrick heals the sick.

Patrick is now around 24 years old and a free man once more. Of course, he is no longer the young Patricius who was stolen away from his family. He has experienced deprivation, fear, loneliness, and also the total self-reliance that brought him to his freedom. His time in Ireland, as a slave, has changed him, and those changes are lodged deep inside him. It must have come as a shock to Patrick to realise that while he had, against all odds, made it home, he still felt like an exile, an outsider. He was caught between his past and his present, and they were two very different worlds.

## The voice of the Irish

This inner conflict begins to haunt him, leading to night visions and dreams he finds difficult to understand or explain. It would have seemed the obvious reaction to everyone – and probably to Patrick himself – that he would fervently wish to never again set foot in Ireland. But now it seems he has brought some of Ireland back with him. In the *Confession,* he writes of a dream at this time that left him *'greatly troubled in heart'.* He sees a man called Victoricus, who was coming to him from Ireland, and this man was carrying a sheaf of *'countless letters'.* Victoricus hands one of the letters to Patrick and it is headed with the words: The Voice of the Irish. Patrick can hear the letter writers' anguished voices:

> *... as I was reading the beginning of the letter aloud I thought I heard at that very moment the voice of those who lived beside the wood of Voclut, which is near the Western sea, and thus they cried out as with one voice: 'We beg you, holy youth, to come and walk once more among us'. And I was greatly troubled in heart and could read no further, and so I awoke.*

Who was Victoricus? We do not know. Perhaps he was an angel emissary, brought forth by the prayers of the Irish? Patrick does not or cannot explain the man in his dream, but he is evidently deeply affected by the vision and the call to return. Does he see himself as a *'holy youth'*, or does this come as a revelation to him? Whatever the truth, awaking from the dream cannot save Patrick from the thoughts and emotions stirring within him.

He has another vision, and this one cannot be ignored. He hears, very distinctly, a voice speaking in a tongue he does not understand, the words echoing through his sleeping mind. And then the voice speaks to him clearly, in his own language: *'He who gave His life for you, He it is who is speaking in you'*. This is an astonishing moment for Patrick – this voice is undoubtedly that of God. At that realisation, Patrick *'awoke rejoicing'*. After this, his path must have seemed clear – he had to give himself over to God's work on Earth and answer the cries of the heathens who were calling out for the Saviour's mercy and love.

## A devoted student

As a boy, Patrick's education would have included the study of the scriptures, including the psalms. He would have been well versed in the works of the Church Fathers, such as Augustine, Cyprian and Jerome. Now, he took up that thread again and decided to enter the priesthood. There are different opinions and theories as to where he carried out his training, but many think it likely that he studied in Britain and in Gaul. There is a homesick moment in the *Confession* when he admits that he would *'dearly love … [to proceed] as far as Gaul to visit the brethren and see the face of the saints of my Lord'*. This suggests he had a strong connection with Gaul and had kinsfolk of some kind there – his *'brethren'* – which means he could have spent time spent there at a monastery.

Gaul covered an extensive area of the Continent, taking in parts of modern-day France, Belgium, western Germany and northern Italy. If Patrick did make his way there to pursue his vocation, it is quite possible he did so to study under the tutelage of St Germanus, Bishop of Auxerre (*c.*378–448). Germanus was himself a successful missionary and knew at first-hand the power of the preacher in converting lost souls and consolidating the Church. Patrick became a priest, and then in time he was consecrated a bishop by Pope Celestine I (*c*.359–432). He was ready to go wherever his pope wished to send him and become an ambassador for God.

Wall painting in Kilkenny Cathedral, showing St Patrick's mission to Ireland from Pope Celestine I.

## Trial

It was at this time that one of the worst events in Patrick's life occurred, one that left a deep mark on him for the rest of his life. We have the outline of that episode in the *Confession,* but it is missing crucial details that would give us the whole story. Nonetheless, the bits we do know provide a fascinating insight, and a very human link, and we know that Patrick was still ruminating on this humiliating experience right into old age.

Patrick describes in the *Confession* how he was *'tested by some of my seniors'*. It would appear that his path to bishop was questioned and almost blocked by some of his peers, who accused him of committing *'sins'* that made him unfit for office. This no doubt came as an immense shock to the man who had given over his life to God and wished to spread the glory of God's name through the work of preaching and converting. From his telling of the story, it seems that Patrick was blindsided by this accusation, and very personal attack on his character and his ability to do his job. There must have been a concerted effort – by an unnamed *'they'* – to bring this serious allegation into the public domain and force it to the point of a trial.

> *They found occasion for their charge against me – after thirty years – in a deed I had confessed before I became a deacon. In my anxiety I confided to my best friend, my mind full of sorrow, what I had done one day in my boyhood, indeed in one hour, because I was not yet in control of myself. I know not, God knows, if I was then fifteen years old; and I did not believe in the living God, nor had I believed in Him from childhood, but remained in death and unbelief until I was severely*

> *chastised and truly humbled by hunger and nakedness – and that, daily.*

The accuser is a friend, and the hurt this gives rise to in Patrick can be heard clearly in the emotion of his words. It might be long in the past as he writes, but there is still a deep sense of betrayal that has never left him. He confided his *'sin'* – he doesn't say what it was – to someone he trusted, and that friend forgave him and insisted that he must be *'raised to the episcopate'* – in other words, all is forgiven, it's in the past, now you have earned the right to be God's servant. But for whatever reason, this friend later brought Patrick's confession of sin out into the harsh light of public debate and scrutiny, with a view to preventing his progression to the office of bishop. Patrick himself cannot understand this very personal betrayal, asking:

> *But why did it occur to him afterwards that before everybody, good and bad, he should put me even publicly to shame [for a deed] for which he had earlier freely and gladly granted me pardon?*

Whatever the charges, or how they were presented or supported, the verdict went against Patrick: *'I was rejected by the above mentioned persons'*. This must have delivered a debilitating blow to him. He starts the *Confession* by telling us immediately that he is *'held in contempt by a great many people'*, which suggests that the outcome of this trial sullied his name for the rest of his life. We are all familiar with the saying that there is 'no smoke without fire', and it's likely Patrick suffered from the association of his name ever after with this scandalous trial. In the twenty-first century, we would refer to it as being 'cancelled' – this sort of rejection that hangs about the person and changes the dynamics of every relationship in their lives, personal and professional.

This view of Patrick – as a man who did make a mistake, who admitted that mistake and received pardon for it, who was then publicly rebuked for it many years later – puts us in very close contact with him. This is very far from the notion of a hero-saint commanding snakes and wrestling hellish demons. This is Patrick at his most human, most like us, despite the centuries that separate us from him. We can relate easily to this very human reaction to human failings and betrayals, and we can feel the real pain and burning embarrassment when he writes of his *'contempt'*.

That sense of deep betrayal saturates his words and it's clear that he struggled to understand and to recover from this heart-breaking experience. The fact that it was a trusted friend who dragged his name through the mud made it all the more difficult to bear. And once he was exposed in this way, other charges were made against him. He writes with an indignant anger that he observed the rules of his office at all times:

> *And many gifts were offered to me with weeping and tears, and I gave offence to the givers; and not [to them only, but also], against my wish, to some of my seniors. But under God's guidance, in no way did I consent to give in to them.*

Reading the *Confession*, it does make the reader wonder if Patrick's primary motive in writing it was to get his version of events on the record in order to counter the allegations that followed him through life. That would be a very understandable reaction: to use the only power he had at his disposal – the power of the written word – to try to exonerate his name and protect his reputation. As there is no record of the trial or the charges or any evidence presented, it could be said that he has achieved this; Patrick's is the only and final word on the matter.

He survived this devastating trial and rejection by turning to his faith, as he always did. On the day he was *'rejected'* and presumably found guilty of some or all of the charges, Patrick goes to sleep a broken man but he is made whole again by a vivid dream:

> '... I saw a vision in the night ...'

*that night I saw a vision in the night, I looked [and] before my face was a writing that stripped me of my honour. And as I looked at it I heard a divine voice say to me: 'We have seen with disapproval the face of ... [designated by name].' Nor did He say 'You have seen with disapproval', but 'We have seen' ... AS if He had associated Himself with me ... This is why I give thanks to Him who in all things gave me strength, so that He did not hinder me from the journey I had decided on, nor from that work of mine which I had learned from Christ my Lord, but rather did I feel in myself no little power from Him, and my fidelity was approved before God and men.'* The solace of innocence and God's love allows Patrick to continue his work and it reinforces his belief, both in God and in his role as one of God's chosen ambassadors. Safe in the knowledge that God believes him, Patrick tell us that

> *I grieve for my best friend, that he should have given cause for our hearing such a statement from the Lord. A man to whom I had entrusted my very soul!*

He may have decided to take the high road and forgive, but there's no denying this public fall from grace rankled very, very deeply. It must have been a sharp cross to bear.

## On a mission

Pope Celestine I (*c.*359–432) was head of an ever-growing Church and he was committed to the expanding of his flock through missionary work. In his *Chronicon,* Prosper of Aquitaine (*c.*390–455) records that in 431 Pope Celestine sent Palladius to Ireland 'as the first bishop to the Irish believing in Christ'. A bishop was only dispatched once priests had carried out the on-the-ground work of conversion, so this suggests there was some sort of community of Christians in Ireland, however small and fragmented. The appointment of Palladius is corroborated by the Annals of Inisfallen, which also record that he arrived in 431.

The annals also agree that a bishop called 'Patricius' was sent to minister to the Irish in 432. This is Patrick's mission, at the request of Pope Celestine. There's no mention of Palladius – whether he

An excerpt from the *Annals of Inisfallen*, Bodleian Library.

fell ill, died, or just gave up on the heathen Irish and requested a less demanding post somewhere else. But it does appear to be the case that Palladius was the first bishop of Ireland, even though Patrick later took over this title. In fact, many historians think that the mission of Palladius was subsumed into the mission of Patrick by later writers. Given that the seventh-century writers of *Lives of Patrick* were much given to embellishment in the name of raising up their saint to the highest heights, this is quite plausible.

Patrick accepted Celestine's mission, and in doing so he accepted exile once again. It must have been an extraordinary moment, to hear his pope ask him to return to the island where he was held captive and enslaved. And yet Patrick accepted to once more become 'a stranger and exile'. Perhaps, after the humiliation of his trial, he was happy to remove himself to a distant place, away from all those who had wronged him? Perhaps he welcomed the humility of the wandering preacher, vulnerable and facing an unpredictable reception? It gave him a chance to show the extent of his love for God, the nature of his character, the depth of his belief in his work and its ability to harvest souls for God. It is interesting to consider all of these possibilities, but Patrick gives us an even more compelling reason in the *Confession*:

> *… for a people newly coming to belief whom the Lord took from the uttermost parts of the earth, as long ago He had promised through His prophets: To you the nations will come from the uttermost parts of the earth … I have set you to be a light for the Gentiles, that you may bring salvation to the uttermost parts of the earth.*

The fact that Ireland was, for Patrick, '*the uttermost part of the earth*', the final point of civilisation, is important here. The Bible taught that once the Gospel had been preached across the whole world, then would come the End of Days with the Second Coming of Christ. So for Patrick, Ireland represented the final stepping-stone on the bridge to paradise regained – a stirring motivation if ever there was one!

Over in Ireland, things weren't terribly changed from Patrick's time there as a teenage slave. The social systems remained intact, still no invaders had uprooted the traditional way of life, and still the druids used their magic to protect and foretell. It is easy to imagine how crucial the druids were to the people, how those stories were part of the fabric of life and death, and how the Irish negotiated those two realms. In the fifth century, life was very vulnerable and people gathered stories and beliefs like protective talismans. The druids fulfilled a need for a sense of certainty: if we light this bonfire and praise this god or goddess, then the crops will thrive and be brought in safely. It was a world in which nature always had the upper hand, so the druids were necessary to bring a sense of balance, a sense of evening up the odds. There was so much to fear – nature, darkness, crop failure, warriors, invaders – that people wanted to feel they had something powerful on their side. The druids responded to that need, their magic creating a psychological barrier against the unpredictable and the uncontrollable.

And yet, the druids themselves knew that times were changing, and that their role was in danger of being challenged and undermined. The Christian missionaries were already on the island, preaching about miracles that could defeat magic. The seventh-century *Life of Saint Patrick* by Muirchú records what is said to be a prophecy intoned by the druids, warning of the danger heading their way across the waves:

> *Adze-head shall come,*
> *With his crooked staff*
> *And his house with a hole in its head*
> *He shall chant blasphemy from his table,*
> *From the eastern part of his house,*
> *And all his household will answer him:*
> *'So be it, so be it.'*
> *When all this happens*
> *Our kingdom, which is heathen, shall not stand.*

The druids were right to feel a sense of dread. On another shore, Patrick stepped into a small boat for his second sea-journey to Ireland. He came now as a man of God, determined to teach the Irish the word of God and tear them away from the influence of their druids. Humans have always needed stories, and respond emphatically to the story of the special being, the chosen one, the magic-worker, the protector. We adore that possibility and what it might open up to us. Patrick would tap into that need, just as the druids did. Of course, these stories always work best when the 'chosen one' fully believes their own story and their role – and Patrick was utterly and completely convinced that he was God's ambassador, fulfilling his destiny. He came across the sea with a new story, and he wanted every person in Ireland to hear it, and give themselves over to its ultimate author: God.

## Did you know?

✤ The oldest map to show Ireland as its own island, separate from the British Isles, was made in 1468 by Italian navigator and cartographer Grazioso Benincasa. The map is part of an atlas hand-drawn on vellum by Benincasa. The island is outlined in bright green – anticipating its 'Emerald Isle' status. It was drawn before the discovery of the Americas by Columbus, when Ireland was – as it was for Patrick – the most far-flung place imaginable, the edge of the known world.

*Freedom and Faith*

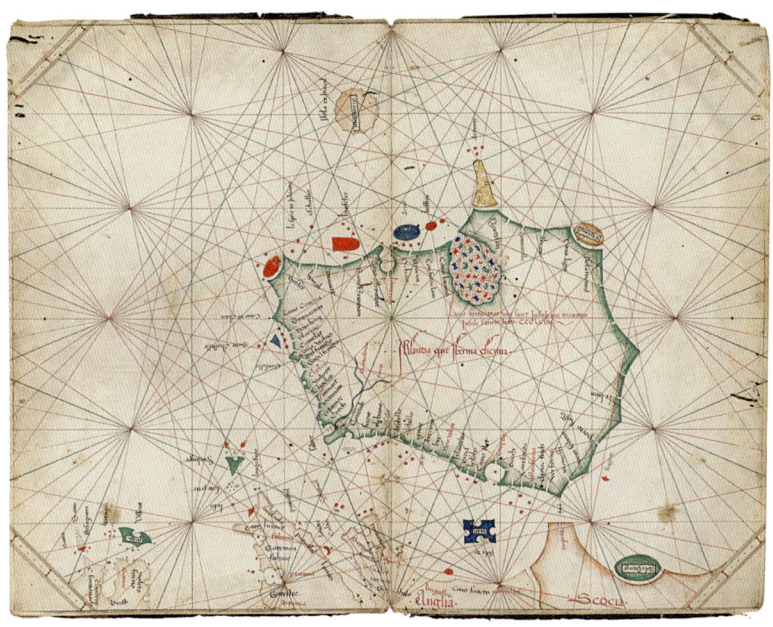

The earliest known separate map of the island of Ireland,
Portolan Atlas, 1468 (ink and colour on vellum).

Detail of the stained-glass window in St Mary of the Rosary Church, Cong, County Mayo, depicting St Brigid holding her lamp.

❖ Patrick is the patron saint and the national apostle of Ireland and of Northern Ireland. But in Ireland he forms part of a triumvirate of patron saints for the country: St Patrick, St Brigid and St Columba (also known as Colmcille). They form their own 'holy trinity' for Ireland.

## Myth vs fact

✜ Patrick has long been portrayed as the man who single-handedly converted the island of Ireland, but this is a myth. The fact is that there were already priests working in Ireland before his arrival *c.*432. The work of Saint Declan, for example, was hugely important in laying the groundwork for Christianity. Declan founded a monastery at Ardmore, in County Waterford, that flourished for centuries. He died in the fifth century.

St Declan's Monastery, Ardmore,
County Waterford.

## CHAPTER 4:
# Patrick the Missionary

*Whence was I afterwards granted that gift so great, so salutary, to know God and also to love Him, even to the point where I should forsake my homeland and my family?*

From *Confession*

Hand-coloured engraving with gold highlights on paper by Adriaen Collaert, 1560–1618.

We can try to imagine what Patrick was thinking as the shores of Ireland took shape on the horizon and he relived the day of his abduction, and of his escape, but what seems certain is that he arrived with a stony determination to save the Irish and herd them into Christ's flock. This would be no easy task. While there were already pockets of Christians on the island, the majority remained Celtic pagans, governed by their chiefs and their druids. The word of God would be a foreign language to their ears.

## Sabhall Phádraig

There are various claims to Patrick's landing spot along the northeast coast, but the most likely and most accepted landing point is at Strangford Lough, a large sea inlet in County Down, Northern Ireland. The traditional story goes that when Patrick landed, he was met by a hostile force led by Dichu of Saul. Despite the attack being an attempt to repel him, with divine assistance Patrick managed to calm the situation and speak to Dichu. It was obviously a persuasive discussion because Dichu accepted Patrick's words and the offer to turn away from paganism and be converted to this new religion. It is said that Patrick baptised Dichu, making him the very first convert of his Irish mission.

For his part, Dichu became a staunch ally and disciple of Patrick and brought him to his nearby territory in the Lecale Peninsula.

In his homeplace of Saul, he gave Patrick a barn – *sabhall* – to serve as his first, modest place of worship: Sabhall Phádraig (Patrick's barn). So Patrick now had a base from which to carry out his missionary work. He would walk miles around Ireland in his bid to convert the population, but whenever he felt weary or worn down by the magnitude of his task, he could return to the tranquillity of Saul and rest there. He developed a love for this place that lasted his whole life, and led him back here when his time came to die.

*Homeless, he landed at Saul. At Saul he found a home and friends. There, Dichu, the earliest of his converts, gave him that barn in which, for the first time on Irish soil, he offered the adorable Sacrifice of the Mass. As it was Patrick's first, doubtless it was his best beloved, Church.*
(Down and Connor Historical Society's Journal, 1931)

Strangford Lough, County Down.

## A hunter and fisher of souls

And so began Patrick's lifelong mission on the island of Ireland. He tells us that he was *'one of the hunters and fishers whom long ago God foretold He would send in the last days'*. This again emphasises Patrick's belief that his work would be the crowning achievement of the Church on Earth, converting the final outliers at the edge of the world and thus ushering in the End of Days and the true glory of God's vision for Man. This belief can only have lent a fiery impetus to his work, a sense of urgency and destiny. He was the last preacher, the one who would gather in the stragglers of the flock and bring them to safe shelter.

Patrick had a distinct advantage in this mission because of his kidnapping and life in slavery. He understood the social system of the Irish, and he spoke the Celtic-Irish language and so could address his listeners in their own tongue. But he was a foreigner nonetheless and trying to force a break with the Celtic past was always going to be a tough sell. He was adept at speaking the word of God and showing the depth of God's love through his own actions, but that didn't grant him immunity from the dangers of preaching an anti-pagan message. In the *Confession* he describes one particularly harrowing incident when he was *'seized, and myself they bound in irons'*. He must have feared he would be killed, but some *'close friends'* came to the rescue and after fourteen days he was freed and able to continue his work.

This unpredictable and dangerous life might have deterred a lesser man – as indeed it might have deterred his predecessor, Palladius – but Patrick was made of stern stuff and refused to be discouraged. He took great comfort from the fact that his life of

St Patrick preaching to villagers.

walking-and-preaching echoed the life of Jesus and he felt safe within the care of God:

> *... for I know as a certainty that poverty and adversity are better suited to me than lucre and luxury. But Christ the Lord, too, was poor for our sake. And I poor and needy as I am, even if I were to wish for wealth, I no longer have it; nor can I judge what my future is going to be; because daily I expect to be slaughtered, or defrauded, or reduced to slavery, or to any condition that time and surprise may bring. But I fear none of these things because of the promise of Heaven, for I have cast myself into the hands of Almighty God, who rules everywhere.*

## Idols and abominations

Patrick's dogged persistence was rewarded with one of the most extraordinary conversion stories in the history of the Church. There isn't a single recorded killing or battle in this slow remoulding of the Irish tradition. From what can be known, it appears that the Irish people who encountered Patrick embraced his message wholeheartedly. He himself says he baptised *'so many thousands of people'* and from all strata of society. He brought about a sea-change in Irish life that would shape the country for centuries to come:

*Consequently, in Ireland, they who never had knowledge of God, but up until now always worshipped only idols and abominations – how they have lately been made a people of the Lord and are called children of God; sons of the Scoti and daughters of their kings are seen to be monks and virgins of Christ!*

Patrick's converts in turn became a powerful network, continuing his work and passing on the baton to those who came after them. So many of the island's most important monastic centres can be traced back to the influence of Patrick's mission. He created the environment in which the Early Christian Church could flourish. It is said that he baptised Enda of Aran (c.450–530), for example, a warrior king who gave over his life to God and founded a monastery out on Inis Mór, the largest of

Harry Clarke's window at St Mary's Church, Ballinrobe, County Mayo.

the Aran Islands off the west coast of Ireland. Tracing his influence down through the years, St Finnian's (*c*.470–549) Clonard Abbey in County Meath, St Ciaran's (*c*.516–549) Clonmacnoise monastery, St Kevin's (*c*.498–618) Glendalough monastic complex and St Comgall's (*c*.516–601) Bangor Abbey all followed the lead of Patrick's work. Inspired by his life of devotion as a missionary, St Columba or Colmcille (*c*.521–597) and St Brendan (*c*.484–578) travelled across Britain and Europe to emulate his work.

Aerial view of Glendalough monastery ruins and graveyard.

The monastic sites founded by Patrick's disciples and successors became the foundation stones for the 'land of saints and scholars', training the faithful and creating beautiful works of art and illuminated manuscripts. This seems a striking part of the conversion of the island – that the Irish embraced not just the philosophy of Christianity but its artistic expression, giving themselves over wholly to the production of books and artworks, to its architecture and to centres of learning. The transformation could not have been more stark: Patrick arrived to a place where writing was lines etched into standing stones, and just *c.*300 years later Irish monks produced one of the most celebrated works in Early Christian art – the Book of Kells. It was an astonishing pace of change, and in itself illustrates just how thoroughly the Irish embraced all aspects of Patrick's religion.

The question, of course, is: just how did Patrick achieve this? A foreigner, a former slave, a homesick man – how did he convert a whole island through word and deed alone, and to such an emphatic extent? Taking from his own writings and what has come down to us through other records, it appears that his success was based on some key factors: his knowledge of the social structure; his ability to speak Celtic-Irish; the story of his own path to belief; and his cleverness in appropriating Celtic traditions and working them into his new story of belief.

## Social structure

Patrick understood the Celtic *tuatha* structure (see p.34) and how the country was parcelled up and governed. Therefore he intuitively understood that the most effective way to approach any community was by going to its leader first. If he could convert the chief, the rest would follow. He did this with great success, starting with Dichu of Saul. He was said to have baptised Conall of Tír Eóghain (Tyrone), who was a powerful Ulster chieftain and therefore an important ally. It must have caused a stir when a man of the ruling elite accepted Patrick and chose to follow him.

An interesting revelation in the *Confession* is that Patrick gave presents to kings, in addition to *'paying wages to the their sons who travel with me'* and also:

> *But you know yourselves how much I paid out to those who wielded authority throughout the districts I more frequently visited. For I estimate that I distributed to them not less than the price of fifteen men, so that you might have the benefit of my presence.*

The former slave speaks the currency of slavery here, weighing up his access to the chiefs in the price of a men's lives. So it seems he paid to gain an audience, and then used his time well to convert the chief and also his sons, offering them a chance to walk with him and work with him. When Patrick walked with a king's son at this side, it was no doubt a powerful visual confirmation of the weight of his words and the value of his belief.

## Language and his story

Patrick would have learned Celtic-Irish during his six years as a slave and shepherd, a skill that would prove essential when he returned to persuade the Irish of the need to convert to Christianity. Of course, he also brought Latin with him, both spoken and written. The fact that he could speak the local language no doubt gave him a huge advantage as he toured towns and rural areas – and it may also have brought people to hear him out of curiosity, to see this 'foreigner' who could converse in Irish.

What he had to tell them about his own journey to God must surely have piqued their curiosity even more and made an impact on those who heard it. A former slave. An escaped slave. A man who had managed the almost impossible and made it back home – only to turn up again years later and choose to live among his former captors. That must have been an unusual story – perhaps even a sensational one – and that can only have helped Patrick to catch his listeners' attention and convince them that any God who could free a slave and inspire him to walk back into the land of his enslavement was a mighty god indeed. It added the layer of incredible story and unmatched belief that must have been uniquely persuasive.

## Christian and pagan

Patrick had a great ability to tune into the beliefs of the Irish people and then graft his Christian story onto those pagan beliefs and sites. He understood the pull of the old traditions, the nature of the sacred spaces, and instead of fighting against them, he simply wound them into his narrative about Christ. This must surely be one of the reasons why his mission was a 'bloodless battle', with not a single martyr recorded in its name. He didn't disparage or contradict, he made the story of God a part of the landscape, so that it felt natural and organic and therefore trustworthy and sensible.

## The wells of baptism

Holy wells provide a good example of the meshing of old and new rituals. Ireland has a long history of sacred trees and wells. One of the Tuatha Dé Danann, the ancient gods of Celtic Ireland, was Dian Cécht, the healer. In Celtic myth, he played an essential role in the epic battles waged by the gods because of his extraordinary well, which could restore a wounded or dead man to life and vigour. This was a form of resurrection, defying death by rising again to fight another day. The wells were long seen as sacred and magical spaces – and that made them an important tool for Patrick. It creates an interesting alignment because by using these wells for baptisms, Patrick was rebirthing his converts into a new life as Christians, echoing how Dian Cécht had rebirthed the dead warriors of old.

There are over 3,000 holy wells across the island of Ireland, and a great many of them are sacred to Patrick. When he arrived into an area and – all going well – converted the top tier of society, he used wells or streams to perform the rite of baptism. In doing so, he claimed that well for Christ and made it 'holy'.

Pinnacle Well, near Ballyvaughan, County Clare.

> *During the second half of the fifth century, when Christianity was displacing paganism in Ireland, the conflict between the old and the new may have been fought out near the sacred wells or in the sacred groves. The sign of the victory of the saint was that he blessed the well and used the water to baptise Christians.*
> (The Holy Wells of Ireland, Patrick Logan)

While the saints wished to change the nature of the well, the usual outcome was that elements of the pagan tradition existed alongside its new holy state. This is why there are so many holy wells that are said to have healing properties – this is a clear example of mixing of the pagan and the Christian. St Patrick's Well in Belcoo, County Fermanagh, was reputed to cure stomach illnesses and nervous conditions. Local historian Joe McGowan, writing in 1938, noted that St Patrick's Well in Leitrim had curative powers: *'For a cure for sore eyes, the water is rubbed on, for a cure for a sick animal, it is given to the beast to drink.'* This pagan-Christian interface is also apparent in rag wells. The tradition, which continues to this day, is to tie a rag on a tree next to the well and pray for a cure or particular outcome. In pagan times, red was associated with magic and the repelling of evil spirits, which is why red rags are often seen at rag wells.

The wells might have become sacred to Patrick, but they still retained their supernatural associations. For example, the well at Granard Cille, in County Longford, was said to have witnessed a battle between Patrick and the druids who were in charge of the well. Patrick defeated them, and the well has been holy ever since. Another magical aspect of these holy wells is their stones that bear the imprint of Patrick, marking where he knelt or stood while praying. There is a place in County Mayo where a triangle is formed by three such stones, each featuring a bullaun (hollow): one lies between Balla and Kiltimagh; one lies near Ballinamore; one lies between Ballinamore and Kiltimagh. The story has it that when you stand within the triangle formed by these three locations, you are safe from war and from death. That speaks of a touching sense of hope – to have a place, blessed by the old and the new traditions, where you may find a safe sanctuary.

Ribbons, cloth and gifts hanging from the branches of a tree at the Holy Well shrine for St Brigid of Kildare.

## Holy Eamhain Mhacha

This approach is also evident in the location of his church at Armagh, in Northern Ireland. While Patrick doesn't mention Armagh in his own writings, he shares a deep and unique tradition on which the primacy of Armagh is based. In documents dating to the early Middle Ages, Patrick is recorded as the first bishop of Armagh and Primate of Ireland, and Armagh is said to be the site of the first stone church he built, *c.*445. To this day, Armagh celebrates its direct link to St Patrick and Armagh is the ecclesiastical capital of Ireland, with a Church of Ireland cathedral and a Roman Catholic cathedral facing each other across a valley.

We must go back into the realm of stories when we seek out the origins of Armagh and Patrick's role in it. The story goes that Patrick wanted to build a church on the hill of Ard Mhacha but was refused permission to do so by Daire, the pagan chieftain of the territory. Daire agreed to give Patrick a site on lower ground, to the east. One day, Daire and his fine horses fell ill and seemed close to death. Daire's men begged Patrick to heal their chief. Patrick anointed man and beasts with holy water, saving their lives and restoring them to health. In thanks for this miraculous cure, Daire granted Patrick the hill of Ard Mhacha and a stone church was built – on the spot now occupied by the Church of Ireland St Patrick's Cathedral.

The hill of Ard Mhacha (the Height of Macha) is close to one of the most important Celtic ritual sites: Eamhain Mhacha (the fort of Macha), also known as Navan Fort. This ritual complex was built in the Iron Age, possibly c.95BC, and is referred to in Ptolemy's second-century AD map of Ireland, the earliest known map of the island. Eamhain Mhacha's centrepiece was a great temple whose purpose remains unclear. Excavations are ongoing, but it is evident that this was a significant spiritual centre and a site of ritual and burial. It appears to have been ritually destroyed and was abandoned by the first century. It is believed this site was the royal centre of Ulster in the Iron Age.

So we see again how Patrick chooses a place that is steeped in history and pagan spiritualism and adds his new layer of belief straight onto it. Eamhain Mhacha featured in the Ulster Cycle, a collection of myths and sagas featuring legendary heroes such as Cú Chulainn and Queen Medb. Macha was a red-haired queen in these stories, the only woman to ever hold the kingship of Ulster,

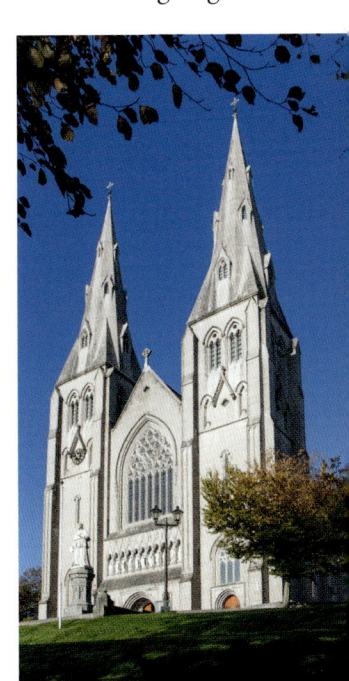

St Patrick's Cathedral Armagh

which she wrested from her uncles through force and cunning after the death of her father. All of this made Ard Mhacha a prime site to show that Christianity provided the new spiritual centre of the island, taking over from a long and magical tradition and replacing it.

The founding of Armagh, and its destiny as Patrick's first and most important site of worship, was described in *The Life and Acts of Saint Patrick* written by Jocelin in the twelfth century:

> *Then Patrick founded, according to the direction of the angels, a city, fair in its site, its form, and its ambit, … And he beautified the city with churches builded after a becoming and spiritual fashion … And in this city placed he an archiepiscopal cathedral; and determined in his mind that it should be the chief metropolis, and the mistress of all Hibernia; and that this his purpose might remain fixed and by posterity unaltered, he resolved to journey unto the apostolic seat, and confirm it with authentic privileges.*

Armagh has fulfilled this vision of its future and centuries later, there stand the two cathedrals, united in their devotion to Patrick.

It is extraordinary to think that Patrick gave the rest of his life to his mission in Ireland. Throughout all his many years working to establish the Church on the island, he was homesick and longed to see *'my homeland and family'* and also to travel to Gaul *'to visit the brethren',* but he never left. This was a choice he made freely, believing that *'Christ the Lord ... ordered me to come and be with those people for the rest of my life'*. Patrick would remain a missionary in Ireland until the day he died.

## Did you know?

✢ Dichu of Saul, Patrick's first convert on the island of Ireland, lived a life of prayer and faith, adopting Patrick's religion and changing his warring ways to devote himself to peace. Like Patrick, he went on to become a saint. The *Martyrology of Donegal* names him as *Diochu of Sabhall,* with a feast day of 29 April.

✢ Another of Patrick's key conversions was that of Conall of Tír Eoghain (Tyrone). Conall was a powerful chieftain and the northwest area was divided and ruled by him and his brother, Eoghan. Conall controlled most of what is now Donegal. What is interesting to note is that the two brothers were sons of Niall of the Nine Hostages – who was reputed to have been the man who kidnapped Patrick from his home as a teenager. He could never have foreseen that a scrawny teenage captive would come back and 'capture' his own sons for God.

## Myth vs fact

✢ The lives of St Patrick and St Brigid (*c*.450–525) are closely entwined in legend. These stories abound and give the lie that the two saints were well acquainted. For example, it is told that Brigid was already at Ardagh, in County Longford, when Patrick arrived to preach. She immediately showed him she was a miracle-worker of the same calibre as him by carrying a lit coal in her apron, dropping it to the ground, and causing a holy well to spring from where it fell. While these stories create a mythical connection, it is interesting to discover that there are some factual links between the two. Brigid's mother was abducted from her home in Britain, just as Patrick was, so Brigid was the child of a slave. Her father tried to marry her off to the king of Ulster – who would have been based close to Patrick's church in Armagh. Perhaps they did meet as they travelled Ireland, but given that Brigid established her monastic community in Kildare, in the southern half of Ireland, that tantalising idea seems unlikely.

*Saint Brigid* by Patrick Joseph Tuohy, Hugh Lane Gallery.

## CHAPTER 5:

# Patrick at the End of his Life

*I Patrick, a sinner and unlearned, resident in Ireland, declare myself to be a bishop. I believe with complete certainty that it is from God I received what I am ... I live for my God, to teach the heathens, even if I am despised by some.*

From *Confession*

Stained-glass image of St Patrick (detail).

Patrick's mission in Ireland lasted *c.*30 years, so he lived out his middle age and old age on the island. He might have been homesick, but he threw himself body and soul into his work and his role as bishop, ministering to his flock. It was during this latter stage of his life that he wrote the two accounts that have, quite miraculously, survived to this day. The *Confession* is the best-known of the two, with its heartfelt record of his life and his joy at being one of God's chosen ambassadors. He describes himself as *'unlettered'* and *'a sinner'*, his humility shining through the words. We meet in the *Confession* a man who is humble and self-sacrificing, with an unwavering focus on doing God's work on Earth. His final testament is that of an old, wiser man who wishes to set the record straight on who he is and what he has done.

## Rebels against Christ

The second document surviving from Patrick's own pen is the *Epistola,* or *Letter to Coroticus.* This is undated, but was likely written earlier than the *Confession* and is about a third shorter than the *Confession*. But it is a fascinating insight into Patrick the bishop, the man at his work. The words and sentiments echo those of the *Confession,* but here we meet Patrick as a fearsome preacher, fiery in his words and delivery, absolutely certain that God speaks through him and therefore that he has supreme authority on the matter at hand. If we imagine him angrily speaking the words, it is easy to understand how he converted a nation – his sermons must have been electrifying and lodged in the mind of any who heard them.

Patrick is writing this letter to communicate his grievous anger to Coroticus, a Christianised chieftain living in either Wales or Strathclyde, depending on which historian is telling the story. Coroticus and his men have murdered or kidnapped newly baptised young men and women – *'white-robed neophytes'* as Patrick calls them – and carried them off across the sea, where these young captives have been brutalised. In his role as bishop and baptiser, Patrick is sending this letter in their wake, expecting it to be read widely and the acts of Coroticus and his men to be condemned far and wide as well:

> *I request with the greatest gravity – whatever servant of God agrees to be the bearer of this letter – that it be on no account withdrawn or hidden from anybody, but rather be read before all the communities, even in the presence of Coroticus himself.*

The letter is unusual in two regards. Patrick states explicitly at the outset: *'With my own hand I have composed and written these words'*. He is telling Coroticus that he hasn't set this task to a secretary, which would have been the normal manner, but rather has taken the time to write it himself, so the words are flowing directly from him. Secondly, the letter does not start with a salutation – which tells Coroticus that he has lost the right to respect, that his barbaric actions have placed him outside civil society.

What follows then is an excoriating attack on the men who breached Patrick's community and harmed his people. Patrick's deep and passionate anger fairly sparks from his words, leaving the reader in no doubt that he is grief-struck and enraged by what these men have done to innocent people. It opens with a declaration that shares a sense of humility with the opening of the *Confession*: *'I Patrick, a sinner and unlearned, resident in Ireland, declare myself to be a bishop. I believe with complete certainty that it is from God I received what I am.'* But then with a flinty, unrelenting anger, Patrick sets out the wrongs that have been committed:

*I have composed and written these words, to be given, sent and delivered to the soldiers of Coroticus; I do not say, to my fellow citizens, or to fellow citizens of the holy Romans, but to fellow citizens of the demons because of their evil deeds. In enemy fashion they live in death ... Bloodstained men bloodied in the blood of innocent Christians, whom I have begotten in countless numbers unto God, and have confirmed in Christ!*

*The day following that on which the white-robed neophytes had been anointed with chrism – it was still fragrant on their foreheads when they were cruelly butchered and put to the sword by those I have named ...*

> *Hence I know not for which I should grieve the more; whether for those who have been slain, or those taken captive, or those whom the devil has grievously ensnared. Together with him they will be slaves in hell in everlasting punishment, because he who commits sin is indeed a slave, and is called a son of the devil.*

Within this trembling anger, it is possible to hear the pain of the former slave. Patrick knows exactly what kidnap and enslavement entails, which is why he is broken by the knowledge of what his young men and women have endured and are enduring. Again and again in the letter he mentions his life in exile, his sacrifice of home, how he lives as *'a stranger and exile'*, and it is clear that this loss is profound for him. In a powerful reflection, he describes this sacrifice:

> *Was it without the inspiration of God, or on my own merely human initiative, that I came to Ireland? Who drove me to it? It is by the Spirit I am bound, to the extent of no longer seeing anyone of my own kindred. Is it from myself there springs the holy mercy I exercise towards that people who once took me captive and carried off the menservants and maidservants of my father's house? I am freeborn by descent: I am the son of a decurion. The fact is that for the benefit of others I sold my*

*freeborn state – I am not ashamed of it, and I have no regrets; in short, I am a slave in Christ to a foreign people for the sake of the inexpressible glory of the eternal life which is in Christ Jesus our Lord.*

Patrick can relate only too well to the young people he has lost to Coroticus. His empathy and his fear for them are palpable. But his aim in this letter is not only to show Coroticus and his men the error of their cruel ways, but also to bring the full might of his bishop's rule down on their heads. This is Patrick at the height of his powers, calling down God's righteous anger and punishment on those who dare to call themselves Christians and then break the very laws on which their faith is founded:

*Consequently let every God fearing person know that they are ex-communicate from me, and from Christ my God for whom I am an ambassador. Parricides! Fratricides! Ravenous wolves gobbling up the people of the Lord like bread on the table!*

He orders every good Christian to treat these men as excommunicated:

*This, then, you holy and humble of heart, is my most earnest plea to you: It is not lawful to pay court to such people, or to eat or drink with them; nor may their alms be accepted, until, through rigorous penance, unto the shedding of tears, they render satisfaction to God, and free the menservants of God and the baptized maidservants of Christ, for whom He died and was crucified.*

The *Confession* shows us Patrick the holy man, the *Letter* shows us Patrick the bishop. Here, he is deeply engaged in the life of his flock, protecting them, advocating for them, taking a hard stance on slavery, ordering his community to make their faith the guiding light of their every thought and action. It is a gift that both of these documents have survived, because they allow us this incredible glimpse into the true nature of Patrick and the depth of his feeling. That deep well of emotion and empathy means he grieves sorely for his lost ones, but he is – as ever – comforted by his love of God. In a heartfelt passage, he makes sure to tell *'Coroticus … and his miscreants'* that their prize is fleeting, and that Patrick has saved these people already, in the only way that truly matters:

*I grieve for you … my dearest ones. But then again, I rejoice within myself. I have not laboured for nothing, nor has my exile been in vain. This crime so horrendous, so unspeakable, has indeed been perpetrated but thanks be to God, my baptized believers, you have gone from this world to paradise. I can see you: you have begun our migration to where there shall not be night any more, nor mourning, nor death; but you shall skip for joy like calves loosed from their bonds, and you shall tread down the wicked, and they shall be ashes under your feet.*

## The Book of Armagh

It is astonishing that these two accounts have survived and come down to us fifteen centuries later, and we have the ninth-century scribes of the Book of Armagh to thank for that. Now held in the library of Trinity College Dublin (and with copies also held in Britain and France), the Book of Armagh is an illuminated manuscript. It is a small, fragile collection of vellum leaves held within oak boards. It measures just *c.*18.5cm in height by *c.*14.5cm in breadth and is *c.*5.5cm thick, but its historical significance is enormous: it contains the earliest known versions of the writings of St Patrick, the *Confession* being the earliest known piece of writing in Irish history.

These copies of original records were written out around the year 807 by Ferdomnach, a scribe living and working at Armagh. So, Ferdomnach is writing long after the time of Patrick, but he is preserving those lost original writings by copying them out and gathering them together. The Book is written in Latin and includes a Life of Patrick by Muirchú, a Life by Tírechán, Liber Angeli

(The Book of the Angel), the *Confession,* a complete New Testament and a Life of St Martin of Tours. For a time, the scribe was forgotten about because the Book came to be known as Canoin-Phadraig (the canon of Patrick) and lauded as being written by Patrick himself. But expert research restored Ferdomnach to his rightful place – he helpfully signed the book on five pages. His death is noted in the Annals of Ulster in 846, where he is described as *'a scholar and excellent scribe'*. If it wasn't for Ferdomnach and the two scribes who assisted him, it is unlikely the words of Patrick would have survived, and their loss would have meant losing

Pencil drawing of the *Book of Armagh.*

sight of Patrick, too, so we – and indeed Patrick – are greatly indebted to him.

At some point in the medieval period a book satchel was made to house the Book of Armagh. This is a beautifully decorated satchel made of thick cow hide with a brass lock. It is also held in Trinity College and is one of only three such book satchels that have survived to the present day.

All of which doesn't explain how this small book managed to survive down through the centuries and through the depredations of the Vikings. That turns out to involve no little amount of luck. The Book of Armagh was in the care of a hereditary keeper, a role passed down through the family line of the MacMoyers of County Armagh. It reached Florence MacMoyer in 1662, but he pawned it for £5, breaking the line of keepers. It now came into the possession of the Brownlow family in Lurgan, and then in 1831 it turned up at an auction house in Dublin. It was bought for £390 and put into the care of the Royal Irish Academy in Dublin. It was in danger of leaving the country after coming to the attention of art collectors, but eventually it was bought by the Archbishop of Armagh, Lord John George Beresford, and he bequeathed it to Trinity College, where it rests to this day.

*Patrick at the End of his Life*

## The death of Patrick

When he was writing the *Confession*, Patrick was an old man and he knew his time was coming to its end. He went back to Saul, the location of his first conversion and place of worship, to prepare to finally meet his God. In fact, some believe he may have written the *Confession* while he was in Saul. A story is told that an angel came to him in a vision to tell him that his place of death was to be Saul, so Patrick made his way to that 'homeplace'.

The traditional date accepted for his death is *c.*461. The *Confession* copied into the Book of Armagh ended with these words: '*Here ends the volume of Patrick, written by his own hand. On the seventeenth day of March he was translated into heaven.*' This is how we know that Patrick died on 17 March, which of course became his feast day.

Altar in St Patrick's Church, New Orleans, with murals by Leon Pomarede.

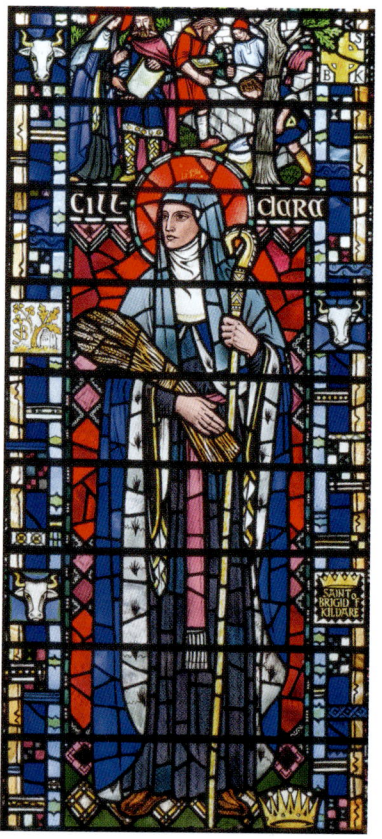

What happened after his death remains a matter of controversy and debate. The tradition that has proven to be most durable is that set down by Muirchú in his seventh-century *Life of St Patrick*. He tells a dramatic story of the battle for the body of Patrick. The Uí Neill wanted to bring the body to Armagh; the Ulaid wanted to bring it to Downpatrick, in their territory in modern-day County Down. Neither side was for turning. The dispute was eventually settled by placing the body of Patrick on a cart drawn by two oxen, and seeing where the oxen brought it. The oxen walked to Downpatrick, which lies just three kilometres from Saul.

St Brigid of Kildare in the stained glass in the church of St Etheldreda, London, by Joseph Edward Nuttgens.

It has long been held that Patrick is not the only saint buried here. This story stems from the twelfth century and the colourful adventures of the Norman knight John de Courcy. He was said to have been granted vast lands in Ulster by Henry II, and he arrived in 1176 ready to fight to take possession. As part of his conquest, he wanted to build a shrine to the three patron saints of Ireland: Brigid, Colmcille and Patrick. Shrines meant pilgrimages, and pilgrims meant money. He was very fortunate to be blessed by a divine miracle, whereby a shaft of sunlight fell on the ground, showing him the forgotten location of Patrick's burial. The remains of Brigid and Colmcille were exhumed and they were laid to rest with Patrick on

St Colmcille in the stained glass in St Mary's Church, Ballinrobe, County Mayo, by Harry Clarke.

the hill of Downpatrick. This 'fact' was recorded in the Annals of the Four Masters in the 1600s, joining the three patron saints of Ireland in death at one place of pilgrimage. This is where the well-known rhyming couplet comes from: 'In Down, three saints one grave do fill, Patrick, Brigid and Columcille.'

There is general agreement among historians and Church authorities that Patrick's remains do not rest here, but to this day Downpatrick (Dún Pádraig – Patrick's stronghold) draws huge numbers of visitors to pay their respects. His 'grave' is a large granite slab that bears the letters 'PATRI' – the others no longer visible – and nearby is a Celtic cross dating to the tenth or

St Patrick's grave at Down Cathedral, Downpatrick.

eleventh century. Now called the Cathedral Church of the Holy and Undivided Trinity, Down Cathedral is an important historic centre that commemorates the life of St Patrick. At the bottom of the hill the impressive St Patrick Centre holds a permanent exhibition dedicated to the island's patron saint – wherever he may rest in peace.

## Did you know?

✤ Patrick is not officially a saint. He was never formally canonised. During his time, the Early Church had no formal system for sainthood, so instead a cult of martyrdom grew up and was usually regulated by the local bishop. The very first saint to be canonised by a pope was Ulrich (*c.*890–973), bishop of Augsburg, who received his sainthood in 993 from Pope John XV. Patrick was too early to receive a formal recognition of sainthood, so his status as saint derives solely from widespread devotion. He is a saint of the people and of their prayers.

✤ There are precious few manuscripts surviving before 700 and the works of Patrick are no different – we only have later copies of them. So what would Patrick's *Confession* have looked like when he wrote it? This cannot be answered with complete certainty, but the Springmount Bog Tablets could show us the kind of 'manuscript' produced by Patrick. These are the oldest extant examples of Latin

One of six waxed, yew-wood tablets found during turf-cutting in a County Antrim bog in 1913, from the National Museum of Ireland.

Traditional turf cutting in a print from 1850.

writing in Ireland and were unearthed in a bog in County Antrim by a farmer cutting turf. They are tablets with wooden 'pages', bound together to form a book or codex, with each 'page' coated in wax, into which a pointed stylus could be pushed to scrape letters. They contain Psalms 30–32 and are held in the National Museum of Ireland. It's possible this is how the *Confession* and the *Letter* looked in their original form.

## Myth vs fact

✤ It is commonly believed that Patrick's writings include the Lorica, or Breastplate of St Patrick, but this is not true. The story goes that Patrick composed the hymn and taught it to his followers as a prayer of protection, and that it could literally protect them by causing them to shape-shift and become disguised from those who wished to harm them. However, much as it would be lovely to have a prayer or hymn from Patrick's own hand, the only writings known to be those of Patrick are the *Confession* and the *Letter to Coroticus*. He did not write down the Lorica, nor did he refer to it in his writing. It first appeared in the early medieval Tripartite Life of St Patrick, so it forms part of the later *Lives* written about Patrick long after his death.

*I arise today through a mighty strength, the invocation of the Trinity, through belief in the Threeness, through confession of the Oneness of the Creator of creation.*

## CHAPTER 6:
# The Patrick of Legend

*However, far from giving the impression that I want to make something big out of something small, I shall (merely) attempt to set forth, bit by bit and step by step, these few of the numerous deeds of holy Patrick ... with the pious affection of holy love ...*

From *Life of Patrick* by Muirchú moccu Machtheni

St Patrick depicted with his staff.

Two hundred years after his death, Patrick had a resurrection of sorts, when he was raised up for adulation, his memory brought out into the light once more and burnished to a high shine with fantastical tales. Now comes into view the Patrick of legend, the Patrick of daily miracles – the most familiar Patrick to us and the best-known stories about him. Here, then, is the 'new' Patrick, with a new mission to fulfil.

> …. and Patrick said: 'In this hour all paganism in Ireland has been destroyed.' And Patrick raised his hands to God because of the druid Lochletheneus and said: 'My Lord, cast out from my presence this dog, who barks at your face and at me; may he go to his death.' And all saw the druid being lifted up through the darkness of night almost to the sky, and when he came down again, his body, frozen with hailstones and snow mixed with sparks of fire, fell to the ground in the sight of all; and [the druid's stone is in the south-eastern parts of Tara to the present day, and I have seen it with my own eyes.

(Life of Patrick by Tírechán)

After reading the words of Patrick himself in the *Confession*, marked by his humility and devotion, reading the legends comes as something of a shock. This is an altogether more aggressive Patrick, quick to anger, flinging about curses with abandon, besting everyone he meets, defying kings and druids, unleashing miraculous power on the unsuspecting pagans, including the ability to raise the dead. The cult of Patrick is a far cry from the *Confession,* but it is also dramatic and colourful and adventure-filled and, for a modern reader, wonderful storytelling.

## Hagiography

In the medieval period, scribes were busy writing Lives of saints that were designed to convince people of God's unmatched power and might, and often to promote a particular Church position. This was the case with Patrick. In the late 600s, two Lives were written by two monks based in Armagh: Tírechán, *c.*660s, and Muirchú, *c.*665–680. Both were works of hagiography, which is a specific literary genre that vividly describes the saints, glorifying their lives, acts and deaths, especially if they were martyred. For the medieval audience, these accounts were truthful and inspiring, showing these men and women as heroic and blessed and unbeatable. It was a heady mixture of biographical fact, folklore, biblical comparisons and sometimes fantastical happenings that must have been utterly spellbinding when read from the altar.

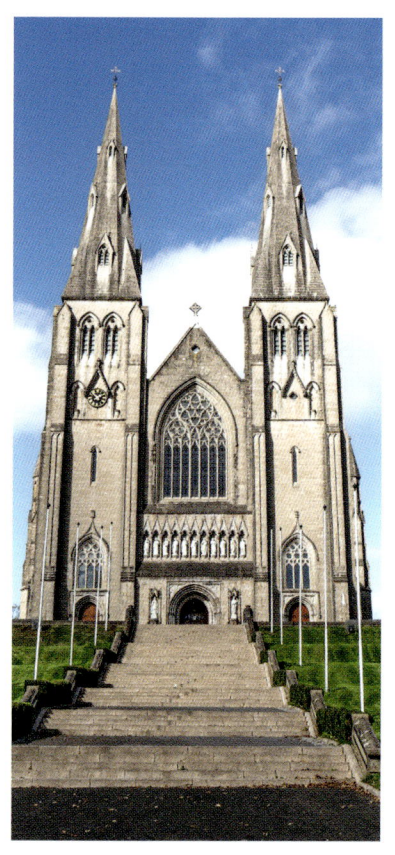

The earliest known Life for Patrick was compiled by Tírechán, but it was largely a list of places the saint had visited and churches he had founded. It was a mapping out of his travels and conversions. Muirchú took this rather pedestrian account and added an exciting layer of story, giving us some of the original mythical stories about Patrick. Both scribes were commissioned by their abbot or bishop to write these Lives and both shared a hidden political agenda in doing so – they wanted to emphasise the role of Armagh in Patrick's

The façade of St Patrick's Cathedral, seat of the Catholic archbishop of Armagh, primate of All Ireland.

ministry and thereby secure its place as the primary church and see on the island of Ireland. Myth-making creates wonderful stories, but it can also be very useful in grounding a particular view in incontrovertible 'proof', and the medieval writers were very well aware of this. They wanted to promote Patrick 'as founder and patron of Armagh' and also to elevate his status as patron saint of Ireland – the man had to match the title. Given that Armagh remains the seat of the primate of All Ireland to this day, it seems safe to assume that Tírechán and Muirchú would be very pleased with the outcome of their efforts.

## And the pagans stood in fear

The Life written by Muirchú depicts an epic showdown between paganism and Christianity. Patrick becomes a man of action, a hero-saint, performing miraculous feats that confound even the druids. The most famous story told by Muirchú is that of Patrick lighting the paschal fire on the Hill of Slane, in direct contravention of the law of the land. This celebrated episode is a powerful illustration of Patrick's work in Ireland, which saw him take on the long-held pagan traditions in order to supplant them with his religion of Christ the Saviour.

## Lighting the paschal fire

There was a huge gathering at the sacred Hill of Tara to mark the rebirth of the year at Bealtaine, the pagan festival that fell on 1 May. Tara was the stronghold of the High King and at this time, in 463, the high king was Loíguire. That night, the hill and palace were alive with people, all awaiting the lighting of the bonfire that would banish the darkness. Everyone in Ireland knew that the first fire was lit on the Hill of Tara and once its flames climbed high, then the bonfires could be lit on the other hills. If any man disobeyed this rule, he would be put to death.

About 21km distant from Tara stood the Hill of Slane, and the one was visible from the other. This was where Patrick stood on this night, which for him was the holy day of the eve of Easter Sunday. Patrick did not hesitate – he lit the bonfire of Slane and blessed its leaping flames. The paschal fire grew brighter and brighter, heralding the resurrection of Jesus, plainly visible for miles around the plain that stretched between Slane and Tara.

Panoramic view from the Hill of Tara, County Meath, of the surrounding landscape, with the Lia Fáil (the Stone of Destiny) in the foreground.

## The Patrick of Legend

There were shocked voices and gasps on the Hill of Tara; fingers pointed towards Slane; *'they all gazed at it and wondered'*. The king called his druids and elders and said: *'Who is the man who has dared to do such a wicked thing in my kingdom? He shall die.'* They all replied that they did not know who had done it, but the druids answered: *'King, may you live for ever! Unless this fire which we see, and which has been lit on this night before the (fire) was lit in your house, is extinguished on this same night on which it has been lit, it will never be extinguished at all; it will even rise above all the fires of our customs, and he who has kindled it and the kingdom that has been brought upon us by him … will overpower us all and you, and will seduce all the people of your kingdom, and all kingdoms will yield to it, and it will spread over the whole country and will reign in all eternity.'*

The king ordered his horses and chariots to be readied and a royal contingent set off, galloping towards the Hill of Slane and the forbidden fire. He brought with him his two most powerful

Statue of St Patrick; looking out from the church of the same name, Hill of Slane, Meath.

druids, Lucet Máel and Lochru. Once at Slane, they ordered Patrick to come speak with the king. Lochru spoke angrily, daring *'to revile the Catholic faith with haughty words'*. Patrick would let no man, druid or not, denigrate his God.

*'Holy Patrick looked at him as he uttered such words and … with a loud voice he confidently said to the Lord: "O Lord, who art all-powerful and in whose power is everything, who hast sent me here, may this impious man, who blasphemes thy name, now be cast out and quickly perish." And at these words the druid was lifted up into the air and fell down again; he hit his brain against a stone, and was smashed to pieces, and died in their presence, and the pagans stood in fear.'*

After this, the king's men moved to attack and kill Patrick. But Patrick called out: *'May God bestir Himself, and may His enemies be routed and His illwishers flee before His face.'* The light died and darkness descended, an earthquake shook the Earth beneath their feet and tore the chariot axles, the horses took fright and galloped away. By the time the noise died down, only the king and three others of his contingent were left standing and alive. They were now very afraid of Patrick. The king pretended to accept Patrick's words, but in his heart he was swearing vengeance against the saint. He did it only to escape and get away from this druid-killer. Patrick knew this. He and his nine companions began walking towards the king, uttering words of holy blessing, and the king watched them approach, but in an instant they disappeared. Now, the king could only see eight deer and a fawn, walking away

*'May God bestir Himself, and may His enemies be routed and His illwishers flee before His face.'*

*The Pocket Book of St Patrick*

St Patrick journeying to Tara in a ninteenth-century engraving.

between the trees. *'And king Loíguire, sad, frightened, and in great shame, went back to Tara at dawn with the few who had escaped.'*

The following day it was Easter Sunday. In the pagan tradition, this was a day of feasting, and a banquet was laid out in the palace at Tara. This year's festivities were subdued as the king and his people mulled over the strange happenings of the night before. All were seated and the doors closed tight. To their astonishment, Patrick and five of his companions walked through the closed doors and stood among them. What could the pagans do but invite this formidable man to join them – and wait for their moment to kill him!

The druid Lucet Máel saw his opportunity. He poured wine for holy Patrick and to the goblet he added a drop of poison. When the wine was served, Patrick blessed his goblet in God's name. The wine froze solid. Patrick lifted up the goblet, turned it upside-down, and the drop of poison slid out, the single liquid drop. Another blessing, and the wine became liquid again. The room fell silent as each one considered the magic this man was capable of working.

Lucet Máel was capable of great magic too, and now he challenged Patrick directly: *'Let us work miracles in this vast plain.'* They went outside and Lucet Máel uttered a spell and snow fell swiftly and softly across the land. It was an incredible sight and the gathering murmured in astonishment.

*And the holy man said: 'All right, we see this. Remove it now.' And (the druid) said: 'Until this hour tomorrow I cannot remove it.' And the holy man said: 'You can do evil and cannot do good. Not so I.' Then he blessed the plain all around, and in no time, without rain or mist or wind, the snow vanished, and the crowds cheered and were greatly astonished and touched in their hearts.*

There were more miracles performed, with the druid and Patrick vying to gain the upper hand. Eventually it was agreed that the druid and Patrick's young disciple, Benignus, would go into a small house and it would be set on fire. The one who survived would, the king agreed, be the one they would adore. Patrick proposed that Lucet Máel would wear Patrick's own holy cloak and Benignus would wear Lucet Máel's cloak. This too was agreed. The two men donned the cloaks and entered the house and the door was shut fast behind them *'and in the presence of the whole crowd was set on fire'*. For the next hour, the fire blazed and Patrick prayed. The fire ate up the wooden walls of the house and the wooden roof and it all collapsed on the two inside.

Detail of the stained-glass window of St Benen (also named Benin or Benignus), St Benin's Church, Kilbennan, County Galway.

When the fire had died down, the smoke cleared, and the people saw Benignus, naked, his druid's cloak consumed by the fire, but smiling and whole and happy. The fire had not touched him. Of the druid, nothing remained save for his bones – and Patrick's holy cloak. And holy Patrick said to the king: *'If you do not believe now you shall die at once, for the wrath of God has come down upon your head.'* And the king was in great fear, his heart trembling, and so was his entire city. King Loíguire summoned his elders and his whole council and said to them: *'"It is better for me to believe than to die," and having held counsel, acting on the advice of his followers, he believed on that day and became converted to the Lord the eternal God.'*

Through these dramatic tales, Muirchú is describing how the fire of Patrick's belief consumed and destroyed the pagan tradition, making way for the word of God to flourish across the island. Patrick out-magicked the druids – they were no match for the power of God unleashed through Patrick. Much

> *'If you do not believe now you shall die at once, for the wrath of God has come down upon your head.'*

as Patrick himself had grafted Christian rituals onto pagan sacred spaces, Muirchú is using a type of storytelling that would have been familiar to his readers: the hero-epic. Patrick is more in the mould of Fionn Mac Cumhaill or Cú Chulainn here, the legendary Irish heroes of the Celtic myths. He is weaving a story around Patrick that will appeal to his audience and feel familiar to them. He places Patrick within the mythical tradition and, by doing so, bends that tradition from within, forcing it to take on the new shape of Christianity. It is artfully done.

## The Tripartite life of Patrick

Muirchú and Tírechán might have felt their Lives were as colourful and fantastical as possible, but two hundred years later a new Life would bring glorious technicolour to Patrick's story. The unknown author of the *Tripartite Life* or *Bethu Phátraic,* written *c.*895–901, used the medieval Lives as

Fionn Mac Cumhaill from an early twentieth-century illustration.

the basis for his telling of the story, but he also allowed himself wonderful flights of fancy to embellish the cult of Patrick. This Life was unique in being the first (that we know of) to be written in Irish, which made it accessible to many more people. It was also unique in being the first to set down the words of the much-loved Lorica or St Patrick's Breastplate or The Deer's Cry. The words are given as part of the story of the paschal fire, retold here and with the added detail that when Patrick and his followers shape-shifted into deer, they were chanting the Lorica – it seems the words held holy power.

This Life starts by identifying the saint as *'holy Patrick, high bishop of the west of the world, father of the baptism and belief of the men of Ireland'*. It goes on to give him five sisters, a mother related to St Martin of Tours, and a childhood filled with model behaviour and minor miracles. This Patrick is holy and blessed from the cradle and he goes on to become a truly epic hero of Christianity, fending off all sorts of demons and monsters. There are two stories here that have become hallmarks of Patrick: the story of his staff, Baculus Jesu; and his fasting on Croagh Patrick.

Croagh Patrick in County Mayo, known as Ireland's Holy Mountain.

## The holy staff or Bachall Ísu or Baculus Jesu

Patrick was travelling across the sea with some of his followers when they saw an island on the horizon. They sailed towards it and made landfall. On the island, they found a house, and in the house was a *'withered old woman'* and a young man. Patrick asks as to the great age of the old woman and the man tells him that they have been on this island *'since the time of Christ. He came to visit us when He was on earth amongst men.'* These, then, must be venerable ancient beings. The man tells Patrick that his coming was foretold by Jesus himself: *'And it is long since thy coming was foretold to us … and God [told] us that thou wouldst come to preach to the Gaeidhel [Irish]; and He left a token with us, i.e., His bachall (crozier), to be given to thee.'*

Patrick refuses to accept the Baculus Jesu, or staff of Jesus. He tells the man that he cannot take it until God himself gives it to him. Patrick stayed at the house three days and three nights, then he went to Mount Hermon. There, *'the Lord appeared unto him, and commanded him to go and preach to the Gaeidhel; and He gave him the Bachall-Isa, and said that it would be of assistance to him in every danger and every difficulty in which he would be.'* During his life in Ireland, this proved to be true. Patrick used the staff to bring forth water from the ground and to fight off demons. In one such story, Patrick arrives at Belcoo, in County Fermanagh, and finds a site sacred to the pagan god of *'harvests, merry-making and human sacrifice'*. He raises his mighty staff and strikes Crom Dubh's altar, smashing it into pieces. This was how he made the site holy and expelled the pagan god forever.

Lough Macnean Lower, near
Belcoo, County Fermanagh.

Pilgrims make their way up the trail towards the top of Croagh Patrick.

## Forty days and nights on Croagh Patrick

In Patrick's time, the mountain of Croagh Patrick, rising above Clew Bay in County Mayo, was known as Cruachán Aigli – the Mount of the Eagle. Patrick made his way to the mountain and then walked to its very summit, bringing him closer to God. There, an angel appeared. Patrick requested that he be granted some special conditions for the people of Ireland. He asks, for example, *'that Saxons may not occupy Eriu, by consent or force, whilst I shall be in heaven'.* The angel grants this. But then Patrick says that he wants to save many souls from hell at the Day of Judgement and that *'I myself may be judge over the men of Eriu on that day'.* The angel refuses. Patrick declares that he will not set foot off the mountain until this request is granted.

Patrick begins a fast, and he observes that fast for forty days and forty long nights. *'Patrick was afterwards with illness of mind in Cruachan, without drink or food, from Shrove Saturday to Easter Saturday, just like Moses, son of Amra; for they were alike in many things.'* At the end of that time, on Easter Sunday, Patrick is subjected to the maddening attack of demons. The mountain and all around was deluged by black birds that swooped and screeched and he could see nothing but their black feathers all around him. Patrick cried out against the demons, singing *'cursing psalms'.* But still they came, swooping all around him. Now, he rang his bell at them and its mighty peal was heard all across Ireland. But still they came. In his anger, Patrick threw the bell at them, breaking it, and at this the demon birds scattered and there was silence once more.

Patrick sat down and wept. The angel returned, bringing white birds to *'chant sweet melodies for him'*. It takes a long time of arguing and refusing to leave the mountain, but eventually the Angel consults with God in heaven and then agrees to Patrick's request. Finally, Patrick walks back down the mountain and returns to the people of Ireland, whom he will judge on the Last Day and save from the fires of hell.

## The Life and Acts of St Patrick

Now we jump forward to *c.*1185, a 300-year leap from the Tripartite Life, to the next crucial instalment in the legend of Patrick: the Life written by Jocelin of Furness. This was written in Latin and English and designed to bring the story of Patrick to the English-speaking world and, in particular, the Norman ruling class. It was written in a style that was familiar to English readers, which made it even more widely accessible.

Jocelin was an English Cistercian monk who was based in Inch Abbey, near Downpatrick. He was brought over to Ireland by

*The Patrick of Legend*

John de Courcy, whom we met in Chapter 5. It was de Courcy who miraculously located the remains of Patrick, Brigid and Colmcille and interred them together at Downpatrick. He also moved the Irish Augustinians out of Down, and moved in English monks from Chester. Among those monks was Jocelin, who came from a monastery in Furness, in Lancashire. He was brought over with a specific job in mind: to write a new Life of Patrick, based on all that had come before, but written to bring the rulers of Norman Ireland into the embrace of the cult of Patrick. This Life was also intended to promote the interests and position of the See of Down.

Jocelin took to his task with great fervour. His approach was logical – a step-by-step telling that brought the reader from Patrick's birth to his death – and it was also epic, building on Patrick's 'hero-saint' image from the *Tripartite Life*. It is

Ruins of Inch Abbey in Downpatrick, County Down.

a compendium of slivers of fact from the *Confession* encased in a dazzling shrine of miracles and folk stories. It couldn't fail to be a page-turner for its Norman audience. The chapter titles alone whet the appetite for the tales of this legendary Patrick: *How he produced fire from ice; Of the Evil-doer Swallowed up by the Earth; Nineteen Men are raised by Saint Patrick from the Dead; The Prayers of the Saint confer Beauty on an Ugly Man; A wicked Tyrant is transformed into a Fox.* This was no dry and saintly account, that much was immediately clear.

There are so many wonderful and unforgettable stories related by Jocelin in his Life, but two stand out as iconic, not only because of their storytelling but because of their legacy as essential elements in the story of Patrick as it has come down to us, centuries later. Jocelin's telling of St Patrick at the Rock of Cashel is really the story of how Patrick ended paganism in Munster – conquering the Rock meant converting the people. And while Tírechán told the story of the fast on Croagh Patrick in a short paragraph, Jocelin bases his version on the long description given in the *Tripartite Life,* regaling the reader with Patrick's torment on the mountain – and giving us the first testimony of Patrick banishing the snakes from Ireland.

## St Patrick's Rock

The Rock of Cashel, in south Tipperary, was the seat of the kings of Munster and is an ancient royal and ecclesiastical complex, now one of the finest and most visited medieval monuments on the island of Ireland. It was to Cashel that Patrick came to speak with and convert the king of Munster, who at that time was Óengus. He was a powerful king, a pagan king, and Patrick knew that if Óengus embraced the word of God, the people of Munster would do likewise.

Rock of Cashel.

When he reached the Rock of Cashel, Patrick found that his holy works and his devotion had preceded him and that the king was eager and willing to talk with him and hear his holy sermon: *'And the king brought him, with great reverence and honour, unto his palace in the city of Cassel, because his mind and his eye had long time longed for him, by reason of the manifold miracles which he knew had been worked by the saint. And at his preaching the king believed in the Holy Trinity, in the name of which he is regenerated in the healing water of baptism.'*

Hundreds of people gathered for the joyous occasion of Óengus' baptism into Christianity. Holy Patrick baptised the king with water, placing his hand on his head to bless him. Then, carried away with the solemnity of the occasion and the force of his own words, Patrick lifted up his staff, the staff of Jesus, and thrust it down towards the ground. As he did so, he pierced the foot of the king. The onlookers were horrified at this grievous mistake, but the king did not flinch, did not cry out. He was stoical and silent: *'But the king, receiving his blessing with ardent desire, felt in his body no pain of the wound, so much did he rejoice in the salvation of his soul.'*

Now Patrick noticed the injured foot of the king. He immediately blessed the wound and healed it. He was amazed by the king's fortitude in bearing this injury, but the king thought it was part of the ritual of baptism and that is why he had accepted it. Patrick rewarded him with a blessed prophecy: *'The blood of any king of thy race who shall sit on thy throne shall never be shed, save of one alone.'* This prophecy came to pass. And Patrick also left *'a tablet of stone … and it is called by the Irish Leac Phadruig that is, the Stone of Saint Patrick; and on this stone, for reverence of him, the kings of Cassel are wont to be crowned and to be advanced unto the throne of their kingdom.'*

This is why Cashel of the Kings is now known as *Carraig Phádraig* – St Patrick's Rock of Cashel. The saint gathered all the souls in Munster or God through his baptism of Óengus, king of Munster. Patrick claimed the once pagan Rock of Cashel for the Christian Church, and it became a revered and important Christian site for centuries to come.

> *'The blood of any king of thy race who shall sit on thy throne shall never be shed, save of one alone.'*

## An epic battle on Croagh Patrick

We heard earlier the story of Patrick ascending Croagh Patrick (see page 127). Jocelin tells us that Patrick's intention was to *'more conveniently pass the Lent season before the Passion; and that there, desiring and contemplating the Lord, he might offer unto Him the holocaust of this fast.'* Just as Jesus had endured the desert for forty days and nights, so Patrick stayed fasting on Croagh Patrick for this same period. Jocelin's poetic description of his fast tells of how Patrick *'... continued and hungered in his body, but his inward man was satisfied, and filled, and wounded with the sweetness of divine contemplation.'*

After this time, he was besieged by demons, who shriek in horror at the sight of the holy man who will destroy their pagan Ireland. And then comes Patrick's miracle of banishment and Jocelin's particular addition to this apocryphal story – his description is worth hearing in full:

*AND the demons grieved for their lost dominion, and assailing the saint they tormented him in his prayers and his fastings; and they fluttered around him like birds of the blackest hue, fearful in their form, their hugeness, and their multitude, and striving with horrible chatterings to prevent his prayer, long time they disturbed the man of God.*

*But Patrick being armed with His grace, and aided by His protection, made the sign of the cross, and drove far from him those deadly birds; and by the continual sounding of his cymbal, utterly banished them forth of the land. And being so driven away, they fled beyond the sea, and being divided in troops among the islands which are alien unto the faith and love of God, there do they abide and practise their delusions.*

*But from that time forward, even unto this time, all venomous creatures, all fantasies of demons, have through the merits and the prayers of the most holy father Patrick entirely ceased in Hibernia.*

In that *'venomous creatures'* lies the undying story of Patrick and the snakes. It's very possible that Jocelin was borrowing from oral tradition here – that a story had sprung up about the demons on Croagh Patrick and this addition reflects that. This could also be the source for mention of it by Geraldus Cambrensis/Gerald of Wales. He

Gerald of Wales (Gerallt Cymro, also known in Latinised form as Giraldus Cambrensis), was a Cambro-Norman nobleman.

lived c.1146–1223 and was a priest, historian and traveller who wrote a famous book called *Topographia Hiberniae* or *The History and Topography of Ireland* (c.1188). Gerald was no fan of the Irish, referring to them contemptuously throughout his book and seeing them as *'a filthy people, wallowing in vice'*. But he does include an interesting note on the patron saint of the island:

> *Of all kinds of reptiles only those that are not harmful are found in Ireland. It has no poisonous reptiles. It has no serpents or snakes, toads or frogs, tortoises or scorpions. It has no dragons ... Some indulge the pleasant conjecture that St Patrick and other saints of the land purged the island of all harmful animals. But it is more probable that from the earliest times, and long before the laying of the foundations of the Faith, the island was naturally without these as well as other things.*

This tells us that the story was current at the time. It is also interesting that in folklore there is a tale that Patrick was confronted by the Caoránach on top of Croagh Patrick. The legendary Caoránach was the mother of all demons, some say the mother of the Devil himself. She was an *oilliphéist*, which comes from *oll* – great, huge, vast, immense – and *péist* – beast, reptile, monster, worm, and it means she took the form of a vast and monstrous sea serpent. The story goes that Patrick fought her with the might of God and he won. He banished the Caoránach to Lough Derg and she took refuge in an underwater cave, where she lives still. This folklore may have reinforced the idea that Patrick banished snakes – because he banished the mother of all serpents. It's interesting, too, that the serpent is the key figure in the downfall of humankind and the loss of the Garden of Eden. Some believe that when the legend was told of Patrick ridding Ireland of snakes, what it really meant was that he rid Ireland of the evil of paganism, that he cast out crude and ungodly beliefs. Given that the island of Ireland has never been home to snakes, there could be truth in this idea.

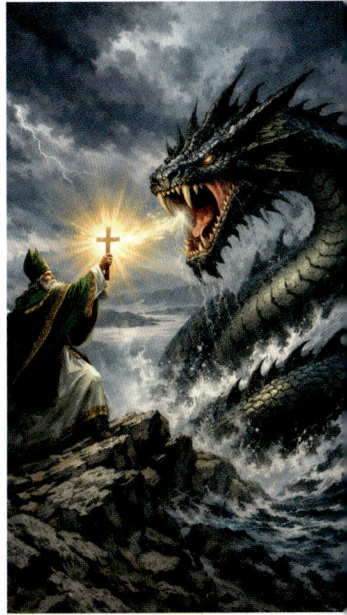

Fantasy illustration of St Patrick banishing the Caoránach.

## Once upon a time

The legend of St Patrick gives a fascinating insight into how stories can be used to create a useful character and to transmit a

set of beliefs. When we trace Patrick from Tírechán to Jocelin, through the various Lives, we can see the evolution of the narrative that was woven around Patrick's life. We are often told about the mightiness of the pen, as opposed to the sword, and here we get to see that unfold in real time, across centuries, in a sort of literary 'Chinese whispers' that builds layer upon layer until the story seems both incredible and true. So much of it is akin to fairy stories: we are in the realm of 'once upon a time', and yet with repetition those stories have become the defining 'knowledge' about St Patrick. A simple story becomes a moral tale, a political agenda, a religious manifesto – and through it all the real Patrick is found, and lost.

Detail of St Ultan in St Macartan's Cathedral, Monaghan, County Monaghan.

## Did you know?

❖ The Lives written by Muirchú and Tírechán made use of a lost book. Before them, there was a *Book of Ultan*, and it was the source they used for many of the stories included in their *Lives*. It is thought that the title refers to the same Ultan who was abbot-bishop of Ardbraccan, in County Meath, and Tírechán's foster-father and patron.

## Myth vs fact

❖ In the mythical story of Patrick and his followers turning into deer, we are told they became eight deer and one fawn. The fawn was said to be Benignus, a young boy converted by Patrick and who became his close disciple. While the story is fantastical, Benignus was a real person and he was converted by Patrick. He went on to have a long and illustrious career in the Church. A Latin Life records him as becoming bishop of Armagh in 455, succeeding Patrick, and dying in 468. Saint Benignus' feast day is 9 November.

## CHAPTER 7:

# Holy Traditions and Sacred Relics

*… without any doubt we shall rise on that day in the glory of …Christ Jesus our Redeemer, as sons of the living God and fellow heirs with Christ and destined to be conformed to His image.*

From *Confession*

St Patrick's Bell Shrine, Armagh.

From the Middle Ages, when the Lives were written to provoke awe and reverence, the cult of St Patrick grew steadily. His memory lay dormant for 200 years after his death, but once the medieval scribes Muirchú and Tírechán retold his story, with their fantastical myth-making style, Patrick became a saint to be reckoned with, alongside St Brigid and St Colmcille. These three became Ireland's patron saints, echoing the triple deities that were so familiar from the Celtic pagan belief system. As the cult of St Patrick gathered pace in Ireland and in Europe, he became associated with various traditions, many of which persist to this day, and with the fascinating practice of venerating saints' relics.

## The tradition of the shamrock

Second only to the story of the snakes, the shamrock is the other most widely known tradition associated with St Patrick. When devotional artworks began to be produced, the snakes became part of his saint's insignia and slithered straight into popular imagination as his greatest foe and their banishing as his greatest heroic act. In Ireland, the shamrock came to occupy the same standing, but it's interesting to note that this wasn't the case across the European cult of St Patrick. The shamrock is a deeply Irish popular tradition – even though it was never adopted officially in heraldry. It doesn't feature in Patrick's own writing or in any of the

*Lives* or in the European images of the saint, but nonetheless the shamrock has become inextricably linked with St Patrick and with the nation of Ireland.

The story behind it is very simple, and temptingly plausible: when he was preaching to the people of Ireland, Patrick plucked a shamrock from the ground and used its three-leafed shape to explain the Holy Trinity of the Father, the Son and the Holy Spirit. He used this tiny plant as a means to explain an intricate theological concept, making it easy for his listeners to understand and to embrace it. However, given that no source or record over hundreds of years mentions this aspect of Patrick's work – and it is a striking image and story, so you would think they would have proclaimed it as part of his legacy – the consensus is that Patrick did not use the shamrock in this way.

Shamrock derives from *seamair óg*, meaning young clover.

There has been much debate – incredibly, hundreds of years of debate – about which exact clover species is shamrock, but it's generally taken to mean the flowering lesser clover or white clover that grows rampant across the Irish countryside. It's interesting, too, that shamrock is mentioned in St Brigid's story, where she decides to base her monastic community in Kildare because of its beautiful stretching plain, swathed in clover blossom. But how did it go from a common or garden plant to one of the most enduring traditions surrounding St Patrick? That process took a few centuries.

The first link came about not in a manuscript, but on a set of coins. In 1645, St Patrick's Coppers or St Patrick's Halfpennies were issued in Kilkenny and these featured an image of Patrick holding a shamrock. They were called 'Confederate coins' because they issued from the Confederation of Kilkenny and were the work of Confederate Catholics who opposed the attempts by Charles I to convert the country to Protestantism through official religious discrimination. The fact that these coins were minted at a time of oppression of the Catholic Irish and confiscation of their lands makes it easy to trace how the image of saint-and-shamrock came to be associated with resistance and nationalism.

After that, the shamrock symbol became more and more widespread and entrenched in popular tradition. This is recorded

An Irish farthing of the reign of Charles II, 1658–1670.

by various writers, particularly visitors to Ireland from England who usually saw it as a deplorable custom. In 1681, Thomas Dineley, an English traveller and antiquarian, haughtily described *'the vulgar'* Irish adorning themselves with shamrock on the saint's feast day: *'The 17th day of March yeerly is St Patricks, an immoveable feast, when ye Irish of all stations and condicions were crosses in their hatts, some of pinns, some of green ribbon, and the vulgar superstitiously wear shamroges, 3 leav'd grass, which they likewise eat (they say) to cause a sweet breath.'*

By now, the shamrock is directly linked with Patrick and with Ireland, but it is still not linked to the story of the Holy Trinity.

*Synopsis Stirpium Hibernarum* title page.

Coloured etching by of a shamrock by M.Bouchard, 1772.

The first mention of that comes in 1726, in *Synopsis Stirpium Hibernarum,* a study of native Irish plants written by Rev. Dr Caleb Threlkeld (1676–1728), who added the story of Patrick to his discussion of white field clover. It might be four decades on, but Threlkeld's description has the same snooty tone as Dineley's: *'This plant is worn by the people in their hats upon the 17. Day of March yearly … It being a current tradition, that by this Three Leafed Grass, he emblematically set forth to them the Mystery of the Holy Trinity.'* That seems to be the moment when the shamrock became St Patrick's holy explainer – and it's a tradition that has only grown stronger ever since.

Today, the shamrock and Ireland are nearly as one in people's minds right across the world. The national airline, Aer Lingus, carries a shamrock on the tail-wing of every plane in its fleet. It features as a decorative motif on many buildings and much street furniture and also in the logos of Tourism Ireland and many sports organisations across the island, including the international soccer and rugby teams. The government registered it as a trademark and fought a court case in the 1980s to defend its right to use it as a national symbol. The government won, further cementing the shamrock as 'belonging' to Ireland. St Patrick may only ever have crushed the shamrock beneath his feet as he walked the *bóithrín* of Ireland, but it has become an enduring part of his legacy – and an essential part of Ireland's national identity.

As well as the tradition of the Holy Trinity story, there are customs that revolve around the shamrock on St Patrick's Day, and we'll look at those in Chapter 8.

## The tradition of the *turas* or pattern

As we saw in Chapter 4, the wells and lakes of Ireland were used by missionaries like Patrick to baptise their converts, giving rise to the phenomenon of the holy well. The sacred water spaces were stolen from the pagan traditions and subsumed into the Christian tradition, creating holy places for devotion and for cures, courtesy of the saint after whom the well was named. There are over 3,000 holy wells in Ireland and a great number bear the name of Saint Patrick. It isn't an even distribution, though, as his wells are seldom found in counties Clare, Kerry, Waterford or Cork, as he doesn't seem to have journeyed that far south/west.

The wells and waterways continued an unbroken tradition of being sacred spaces, with Patrick's God replacing the ancient pagan gods. People once left offerings for river goddesses, like Boann (Boyne) and Sionann (Shannon), but now they came to the wells on the saint's feast day to perform a *turas* or pattern. This tradition was widespread right through the twentieth-century, and while it has fallen away somewhat now, it is still practised in many places. When visiting a holy well, it's common to find a rag tree nearby – usually a hawthorn, adorned with ribbons fluttering in the breeze, each one representing a prayer. There's a good example of this in County Clare, at St Brigid's Well in Ballysteen, near the Cliffs of Moher.

The word *turas* means journey, and it reflects the 'journey' the pilgrim made around the holy well site. It was once a specific pattern that was followed – although most people wouldn't perform the full *turas* nowadays. But for those who wished to honour St Patrick and receive his blessing, they completed a circuit of 'stations' around the well. This involved starting with five decades of the Rosary, before approaching the well, kneeling and reciting more prayers. Then the pilgrim walked right-hand-wise around the well, praying all the while, and repeated this walking pattern three times. They then dipped their hand in or drank the water of the well, blessing themselves with the water. If the pilgrim had a specific prayer, they would tie a ribbon to the rag tree and recite prayers there too. Some pilgrims chose to complete the *turas* on their knees, on hands and knees, or barefoot.

Another common feature of the wells is a stone with hollows, said to be the imprints of the saint's foot, or head, or knees, or hands. In one amusing case, at Cross Patrick in Killala, County Mayo, there's a stone bearing the imprint of St Patrick's bottom, which was obviously as holy as the rest of him. There is a tradition associated with these stones that if a pilgrim puts the water of the well into the hollow of the stone, it increases the water's healing power. Many of the wells were said to cure ailments. For example, one of the largest wells, St Patrick's Well in Clonmel, County Tipperary, was said to have the cure for sore lips and eyes, and people visited the one at Patrickswell town in County Limerick to cure toothaches.

Of all the wells dedicated to Patrick around the island, perhaps the most intriguing is Struell Wells in Downpatrick, County Down, close to what is said to be the saint's final resting place. Here, it is a midsummer pilgrimage, rather than his feast day, that is marked. The *turas* started on the evening of 23 June at Downpatrick, where the pilgrims attended Mass before taking a handful of clay or a stone from St Patrick's grave and carrying it to Struell. There, they performed the pattern of prayer, usually on their knees, and added their clay or stone to the heap. The water running through the site is the River Slán, which means health, and it is renowned for its curing powers.

This site is unusual – and very atmospheric – because it lies within a secluded valley and has two wells topped with stone corbelled huts and two stone bathhouses – one for men and one for women. This is said to be the only site where pilgrims bathed fully in the well waters as part of the *turas* between the seventeenth and nineteenth centuries. In an account of 1744, Walter Harris noted that: '... *the largest of these vaults is the most celebrated, being in dimensions sixteen feet and a half by eleven, and is more particularly said to have received Patrick's Benediction. In this they bathe the whole body, there being a commodious Chamber fitting up for dressing and undressing.*' It was said that Patrick himself visited from Saul and bathed in the waters and blessed them. This event features in St Fiacc's Hymn, which is part of the Tripartite Life:

> *In Slan, in the territory of Benna-Bairche, hunger or thirst possessed him not.*

The bathhouses at Struell Wells.

*Each night he sang a hundred psalms, to adore the King of Angels.*

The site also featured a rock outcrop called St Patrick's Seat. This was the hill pilgrims ascended on their knees as part of the pattern. They had to make their way up to the seat, then circle it on their

> 'Relics in the Church have always received particular veneration and attention because the body of the Blesseds and of the Saints, destined for the resurrection, has been on earth the living temple of the Holy Spirit and the instrument of their holiness.'
>
> *Relics in the Church: Authenticity and Preservation*, Rome 2017.

knees seven times, reciting prayers – their poor knees and backs no doubt aching from the effort. During its heyday, huge crowds gathered at Struell to perform penance and to ask for a cure. The pilgrimage in this form no longer exists, but people do still visit Struell from time to time seeking cures.

## Sacred relics

The practice of the veneration of relics blazed through Europe in the Middle Ages, fostering a burning interest in, and a market for, saints' relics. The saints came to be seen as intermediaries between man and God, able to expedite prayers and intercede for good outcomes. The medieval writers turned them into miraculous beings, and so even their bodies became sites of miracle and therefore worthy of veneration.

The Church defined three classes of relic: first-class relics were actual body parts of a saint or a fragment of the True Cross;

second-class relics were a saint's clothes or personal belongings; third-class relics were objects that had come into contact with a first- or second-class relic, like a saint's rosary beads. As the cult of the relic became more popular in Ireland and Britain, precious relics were often stored in a custom-made reliquary. These were metal or wood containers that were sometimes in the shape of the relic they contained, so they might have been shaped like an arm or a hand, for example. These enshrinements could be very useful in religious, political and economic terms, creating religious sites that drew pilgrims – and their purses – from all across Europe.

The cult of St Patrick was very well developed in the Middle Ages. He was known across Europe and there was huge interest in his life and miracles, thanks to the various Lives. The earliest reference to Patrick's relics is in the Annals of Ulster, which refers to a lost book in an entry for 552: *'I found it written in the Book of Cuanu that the relics of Patrick were enshrined sixty years after Patrick's death by Colmcille. Three valuable relics were found in the tomb, the chalice, the Gospel of the Angel and the Bell of the Will.'* The Annals tells us that an angel appeared to Colmcille and told him to send the chalice to Down, the bell to Armagh, and for Colmcille himself to keep the gospel. This testimony was reinforced by Tírechán in his seventh-century *Life*: *'Colmcille at the inspiration of the Holy Spirit, opened the tomb of Patrick, proving that it is in Saul of Patrick, that is, in the church beside the sea.'*

This tradition was strengthened by John de Courcy *c.*1176, when he declared that he had found the holy remains of Patrick, Brigid and Colmcille and reunited them in a single grave and shrine at Downpatrick. This was an audacious move, creating a 'super shrine' that was guaranteed to become an essential site of pilgrimage for pilgrims from many different countries. The importance of Patrick's first-class relics continued for centuries. In 1942, a special Vatican department transported fragments of Patrick's bone to New York inside a small reliquary. It was sealed inside the high altar of St Patrick's Cathedral in Manhattan, New York. So right into the modern era, relics still have the power to confer status on the churches that house them.

And it wasn't confined to the body of Patrick and its place of burial. What was crucial to his legacy was his movable relics, such as his bell and the shrine of his tooth, which could be passed down from generation to generation and brought from place to place. These relics were safeguarded by different families, who hid them, bequeathed them and ensured they were preserved down the centuries. We have those families to thank for the St Patrick relics we can still see and visit today.

## St Patrick's Bell and the Shrine of the Bell

The bell of St Patrick (Clog Phádraig) is one of the relics said to have been buried with him, then removed by St Colmcille. It is made of iron and bronze, with an iron clapper. The hand-bell is a humble, simple, everyday object, but *c.*1100 a shrine was made to house the bell, and this shrine is beautifully ornate. It is decorated with swirling beasts and snakes and birds, inlaid with silver plate and gold filigree. The maker left an inscription on its surface, telling us that it was commissioned by Domhnall Ua Lochlainn, who was high king of Ireland between 1094 and 1121, that Condulig Ua hInmainen and his sons crafted the bell, and that Cathalan Ua Maelchallain was the keeper of the bell. The Ua Maelchallain (Mulholland) family kept the shrine and bell safe for generations. It finally came into the

A replica of the Shrine of St Patrick's Bell.

possession of Henry Mulholland, who had no children, so he passed it into the safekeeping of his friend, Adam McClean in 1819. On his deathbed, McClean donated it to Dr Todd of Trinity College Dublin, who in turn sold it to the National Museum of Ireland for £500. The bell and its beautiful shrine are still on display in the museum.

## The Shrine of St Patrick's tooth – Fiacail Phádraig

This tiny wood and copper alloy reliquary was said to hold the tooth of St Patrick. It is decorated in bronze and silver with settings of crystal, glass and amber. The tiny figures in relief depict Patrick, St Benon, St Brendan and St Colmcille, among others. An inscription tells us that 'Thomas de Bramighen, Lord of Athenry, caused me to be ornamented in this part'.

Patrick seemed to make a habit of losing teeth, and while this shrine is for a tooth reputedly found at Killaspubgrone, County Sligo, there is a lovely description in Jocelin's Life of another tooth lost:

> *AND on a time the saint, with his holy company, passed over a certain, river named Dabhall ... And approaching the water, he washed his hands and his mouth, and with his most pious fingers he rubbed his gums and his teeth; but through age or*

*infirmity one of his teeth, by chance, or rather by the divine will, dropped out of his mouth into the water; and his disciples sought it diligently in the stream, yet with all their long and careful search found they it not. But in the darkness of the night the tooth lying in the river shone as a radiant star, and the brightness thereof attracted all who dwelled near to behold and to admire. And the tooth so miraculously discovered is brought unto the saint, and he and all around him offer thanks to the Almighty, who had brought this thing to pass …*

It is incredible that such a small reliquary has made it down through the generations. In the early nineteenth century it was held by a man named Reilly, and he did a great trade in cures using the tooth. Thankfully, the Abbot of Cong heard about this 'miracle-worker' and rescued the shrine and tooth from him, and gave it to the Royal Irish Academy. It is now on display in the National Museum of Ireland.

## St Patrick's reliquary bust

There is one relic that is quite unusual in Ireland, and it can be seen in the Hunt Museum in Limerick. It is thought to have been made in France and is a bust of the saint, made of silver, with a hinged top and a grille through which the relic – probably a piece of bone

– would have been viewed. It sits on a base inlaid with nine crystals. The inscription translates from Latin as: Lord James Butler, Earl of Ormond, Justiciar of the island of Ireland, had me made in honour of St Patrick.

## The shrine of the hand

This shrine is of the type where the shrine is made in the shape of the part of the body it encases. This hollow arm and hand are fashioned in the shape of a hand giving the sign of the episcopal blessing, as St Patrick would have done countless times. It is made of silver, with green, blue and black domed glass studs. Like the bell shrine, it is decorated with animal motifs, and a ring with a purple stone is soldered onto the second finger. It is empty now, of course, but tradition holds that it was once on the high altar at Down Cathdral and did contain Patrick's hand and arm, taken from their resting place when John de Courcy disinterred Patrick's remains. It can be seen at the Ulster Museum, where it is on long-term loan from the Diocese of Down and Connor.

## Domhnach Airgid

This is a book shrine, made of yew-wood, copper and silver, that was found in Clones, County Monaghan. It was reworked over the centuries, but its first phase dates to the eighth century, when it is believed to have been made as a casket to hold relics. It survived the generations and in the nineteenth century, the shrine was opened. Inside, there were badly damaged vellum pages from an illuminated manuscript of the Gospels, written in Vulgate Latin. No one knows where exactly the manuscript came from, or when it was placed in the shrine, but it is older than the shrine itself. The association with St Patrick stems from the fact that he is one of the saints depicted on the shrine and there is a mention of Domhnach Airgid in the medieval Lives. The expert opinion is that it is unlikely to be a gospel owned by Patrick, but the popular belief is that it is a sacred relic of his belongings. It is held in the National Museum of Ireland.

## Did you know?

✤ Ireland has three patron saints: Patrick, Brigid and Colmcille (who was also known as Columba). Patrick's feast day on 17 March has been marked by a bank holiday since 1903. Colmcille's feast day on 9 June has never been afforded this level of celebration. But in 2023, St Brigid joined St Patrick when her feast day, 1 February, was designated a bank holiday in Ireland.

## CHAPTER 8:

# St Patrick in Art

*... great profit is derived from all sacred images ... because the miracles which God has performed by means of the saints ... are set before the eyes of the faithful; that so they may ... be excited to adore and love God, and to cultivate piety.*

From Council of Trent, 1545-1563

Patrick accidentally piercing the king's foot with his staff, *Legenda Aurea*, Jacobus, de Voragine, c.1229–1298 (detail).

There is a long history of St Patrick appearing in artworks, and it tells an interesting story about the role of art in cementing a saint's holy status and in authenticating their miraculous abilities. For the Church, a painting or a mural or a stained glasswork can relate a powerful story without words, which was essential when preaching to people through the centuries who were illiterate. They could listen to the words of God through their priest, but it was so much more effective to show them a dramatic story played out through images. This is the basis of every piece of religious art, both public and personal, such as scapulars or medals, that became part of people's lives and faith.

## High crosses

The very earliest works of art depicting St Patrick are high crosses, and the oldest of these is the seventh-century decorated cross at Carndonagh, on the Inishowen Peninsula in County Donegal. In fact, this St Patrick's High Cross, also known as Donagh Cross, is one of the earliest Christian crosses outside of mainland Europe. It is said to mark the spot of a monastery founded by St Patrick, but there are no remains to prove this and very little information about the site. The high cross is the only evidence left to us.

It is carved from red sandstone and engraved with patterns from Celtic artwork, such as interlacing, alongside Christian scenes, including the crucifixion. It stands 3m/10ft high and is flanked by two smaller pillar stones on either side, all of them protected now by a wooden canopy. The pillar stones are also carved with figures, and one of them is a figure holding a bell and a book or satchel, with a staff at his feet. These are the common emblems of a bishop or abbot. Could they refer to St Patrick? Or does this figure simply commemorate the many pilgrim preachers who walked throughout Ireland? It is impossible now to know for sure.

There is a ninth-century Celtic high cross at Kells in County Meath that is inscribed with the words: *PATRICII ET COLUMBAE CRUX,* meaning The Cross of Patrick and Columba. It stands 3.3m/10.8ft high and is one of five early high crosses in the town, marking the site where a monastery was founded in *c.*804 by monks from Iona, St Colmcille's/Columba's celebrated abbey. The Book of Kells may be more famous, but these crosses are considered masterpieces. They are intricately carved with detailed biblical scenes that wordlessly retell the key episodes, such as Daniel in the lions' den, the crucifixion, the last judgement, and the fall of man. They were the work of Early Christian monks who carved them with great skill in order to honour the Irish saints and encourage devotion to them as ambassadors of God.

Patrick accidentally piercing the king's foot with his staff, *Legenda Aurea,* Jacobus, de Voragine, *c.*1229-1298 (detail).

## The oldest image

The oldest known image that exists of St Patrick is in a thirteenth-century manuscript of the *Legenda Aurea* (Golden Legend) by Jacopo de Voragine, kept in the Huntington Library in California, USA. The manuscript was a collection of saints' lives that was incredibly popular during the Middle Ages, reproduced thousands of times and read eagerly all over Europe. It had such a wide-reaching effect that it is credited with shaping medieval literature and art, and inspiring countless artists and writers across many countries. The Golden Legend is a cornerstone of the medieval imagery of the saints, and the power and influence of the Early Church.

In the story of St Patrick, an illuminated image accompanying his story shows the moment when Patrick unwittingly pierced the foot of King Óengus with his staff as he baptised him (see page 168). The king's shod foot is sprouting red blood where Patrick's staff has speared right through, but the king sits placidly, not reacting. This first Patrick is robed in a blue monk's habit with a hood. This is long before the colour green became synonymous with the 'emerald isle' and its patron saint. Patrick is in blue, with a shaved head, tonsure and short beard, and his halo glows reddish-orange around him. He is the barefoot pilgrim, the monk, the devoted baptist. This image is much closer to the reality of how Patrick would have looked and dressed than the images that are so familiar to us nowadays.

The oldest known Irish image of St Patrick is the Shrine of the Tooth of St Patrick, or Fiacail Phádraig (also see page 156). This is a little wooden case, made in the twelfth century and renovated in the 1370s, and said to hold a tooth of the saint. It features the carved images of a

Shrine of St Patrick's Tooth, National Museum of Ireland.

number of saints, including St Patrick. Here, he is shown wearing a low mitre (bishop's hat) and he is clean shaven, holding a staff.

## The signs of a saint

As the Middle Ages progressed, and then the Renaissance flourished, religious art became more and more important and a new visual shorthand was created that allowed the faithful to 'read' the artworks. So when a painting featured, for example, a peacock, they knew that referred to immortality, and if it featured a fire, that referred to the Holy Spirit. In the same way, the saints were given their own objects or symbols so they were immediately recognisable, such as St Peter being depicted with a set of keys, to represent his role as the keeper of the gates of heaven. For those who had experienced red martyrdom, i.e. they had been killed for their beliefs, the object usually invoked the manner of their death. So a man holding his own flayed skin was clearly St Bartholomew, while a woman holding her breasts on a plate could only be the martyred St Agatha.

In the case of St Patrick, he had experienced white martyrdom, meaning that he lived a selfless life of sacrifice and devotion – but never suffered physically in the name of his faith. His saint symbols were things that were intimately connected with his story – chiefly his staff, his bell, the shamrock and the snakes. We have already encountered his bell (see page 155) and know well the symbols of the shamrock and snakes. One of the earliest images of St Patrick and the banishing of the snakes occurs on a beautifully carved crozier. An inscription in Latin tells us that: *'Cornelius O'Dea, Bishop of Limerick, caused me to be made AD 1418, and in the eighteenth year of his consecration'*. This is the O'Dea Crozier, standing about 2.2m high and made of silver. It features the Blessed Virgin and the Angel Gabriel and various saints – one of those being St Patrick. He is shown holding two sticks or staves that he is using to cast out a reptile at his feet. In this way the image of his 'miracle' is recorded and preserved and passed on.

However, it is the staff that is perhaps St Patrick's most significant object of association. We heard the story of how he acquired his staff on page 124 – in the *Tripartite Life,* it is revealed that the staff came from God and was gifted to Patrick. This is why St Patrick's crozier was called the Baculus Jesu – the staff of Jesus – and in Irish, *Bachall Ísu*. There could be no holier relic, and it was venerated as a divine object for centuries. It became a staple part of depictions of St Patrick from earliest times. When John de Courcy minted coins featuring the name of Patrick in the twelfth century, the cross-staff was represented as a symbol of the saint. It is there, too, on the earliest Irish image – the Shrine of the Tooth.

And it has an important role in the earliest image we have, from the *Legenda Aurea,* where it is piercing the foot of the stoic King Óengus.

So from those earliest times, this unique relic formed part of Patrick's identity, and became a simple way to mark him out in religious imagery for the faithful. It features prominently in a compelling depiction in a manuscript from 1451, where St Patrick is holding it firmly aloft while around him demons cavort, delighting in the torture of sinners. The crozier was said to have extraordinary powers to cast out evil and to protect. This is seen again in a colourful print from 1603 showing *Scenes from the Life of Saint Patrick,* by the Flemish engraver Adriaen Collaert (1560–1618) (see page 67). Here, St Patrick holds the staff while a collection of creatures – scorpion, dragon, lizard and snakes – cower at his feet. The miraculous *Bachall Ísu* can ward off the unwanted, whatever form it takes.

## Creating St Patrick

All of this symbolism and devotional imagery came together in a definitive portrait that has proven to have long-lasting influence on how we see St Patrick to this day. Thomas Messingham, a native of County Meath, became Superior of the Irish College in Paris *c.*1621. There, in 1624, he produced a book called *Florilegium Insulae Sanctorum* (a collection of Irish saints' lives). The frontispiece of the book had three images: Saints Columba, Patrick and Brigid. This shows St Patrick in full bishop's regalia, staff in hand, a knot of snakes writhing beneath his feet. In the print of 1603, he is shown clean shaven and quite youthful – but here, he becomes St Patrick, the man of authority. His mitre (bishop's hat) is tall, his beard is long and full, his clothes are magnificent, his bearing is every inch the stately ambassador of God.

This particular portrait was very influential because it was so widely copied. It appears in the 1809 edition of Jocelin's *Life* published in Dublin, for example. But by far its greatest influence came when it was reproduced on coins in the 1700s, making this image of Patrick widely seen and available – not treasured away in holy books that the average person never got to see. As a result, it became the accepted image of the man – and that's the case right until the present day. This St Patrick wouldn't be familiar to people of the fifth century, but he is easily and immediately recognisable to us today.

Over time, St Patrick and his shamrock became iconic symbols of Irish and Irishness, just like the colour green. In the rebellions of the seventeenth century, green flags with harps began to be flown by

St Patrick's Cathedral of the Church of Ireland, Armagh, County Armagh.

those fighting against Protestant rule. In the eighteenth century, the Society of United Irishmen wore green clothing as a symbol of their resistance, immortalised in the rebel ballad, 'The Wearing of the Green', with its stirring chorus lines: '*They're hanging men and women / For the wearing of the green.*' The colour orange came to be associated with the Protestant tradition on the island, while the colour green became associated with the Catholic tradition. Into this mix was added St Patrick and the shamrock, to become the trinity of symbols that now represent Ireland right around the world: the colour green, the patron saint, the shamrock. That association continues as strong as ever into the twenty-first century.

It is interesting to see the contrast in how St Patrick is presented in the Protestant Church. He is a saint who is venerated in both the Protestant and Catholic tradition, so his image appears in churches right across the island. The Catholic imagery is often lush with colour and symbolism and splendid bishop's regalia – but the Protestant

*St Patrick in Art*

imagery is altogether more humble. There is a good example in the stained glass of Armagh Church of Ireland Cathedral. Here, St Patrick appears middle-aged, with a short goatee-style beard, and a determined expression. He wears a tunic that is more befitting a monk than a bishop, and it is plain white. He wears a cloak over his tunic, which is purple and gold. He is wearing Roman sandals and is standing on a swathe of shamrock. His staff looks like a shepherd's crook and is gripped firmly in his hand. This is Patrick as an unassuming, devoted pilgrim preacher – very different from Messingham's figure of authority.

## 'Our' St Patrick

So, what does the art of St Patrick look like in the twentieth and twenty-first centuries? The saint is still an important topic for many artists, but now we see interesting new approaches to his image in artworks. There

St Patrick stained-glass window (detail), Church of Saints Peter and Paul, Athlone.

is a strong tradition of stained glass depicting St Patrick over the past century. Richard King created a window for St Joseph's Church on O'Connell Avenue in Limerick City in 1932 that gives the saint a modernist twist. He is ablaze in green, his vestments shining emerald, a green mitre on his head and a large shamrock adorning his chest. But his face is long and strongly shaped, the beard short, and the eyes large and expressive. The symbols tell us this is Patrick, but the artist has give him a modern expression.

Ireland's foremost and most famous stained-glass artist is Harry Clarke (1889–1931). He was born on St Patrick's Day, aptly enough, given that St Patrick is the subject of some of his most celebrated artworks. In 1918 his nine windows for the Honan Chapel at University College Cork were unveiled, and generated awe and delight throughout the art world. The delicate detail, rich and vibrant colours and layered symbolism would become Clarke's trademark style. His Patrick in Honan Chapel is enrobed in sumptuous green and holding up a shamrock. These colours are echoed in a window made in 1925 for St Michael's Church in Ballinasloe, County Galway. Patrick is again in vibrant green robes, but here his low mitre is blue. His arms are outstretched, towards his people, as he preaches the word of God.

Harry Clarke died young, at only 41 years of age, and St Patrick

St Patrick detail, Harry Clarke, Honan Chapel, stained glass.

featured again in what would be his final work: *The Last Judgement* at St Patrick's Catholic Church in Newport, County Mayo. This is three window panels, above the altar on the east wall of the church. Canon McDonald commissioned the work – and then paid the £800 bill with his own life insurance policy. This three-panel work is vivid, richly coloured and dramatic. The first window shows Mary, seated, and surrounded by heavenly beings. In the centre, a crimson-robed Christ with a glowing golden halo stands in judgement of the souls of the dead, hands held out to show the stigmata. The final panel shows those souls who have been damned being pushed down to hell. Above them sits Patrick, resplendent in blue and green robes, a long beard, his staff by his side. He is among the saintly brethren, his rightful place. Clarke could not have known this was his final work, but it is interesting that he put himself into the scene. Below St Patrick, among the damned, there is an eye-catching green figure, upside down, his head towards Hell. This doomed figure is a self-portrait by the artist.

## St Patrick Centre, Downpatrick

In 2001 a new exhibition space opened in Downpatrick and became – and remains – the only permanent exhibition on the life of St Patrick in the world. The stunning building is a short walk from Downpatrick Cathedral and the grave said to be Patrick's final

*St Patrick in Art*

resting place. This is the twenty-first-century approach to describing and recording the life and work of St Patrick – and a far cry from the illuminated manuscripts of old. The Centre has an interactive multimedia exhibition, including an IMAX cinema, that walks visitors through the story of Patrick.

## Did you know?

✢ The tallest statue of St Patrick in the world is that on top of Slieve Patrick, built in the 1930s to mark the 1500th anniversary of Patrick's arrival in Ireland. It stands 47 feet/14m tall and when standing at its foot, you can enjoy sweeping views across Strangford Lough. It symbolises how Patrick is honoured in both the Protestant and Catholic traditions: his robes are those of the Roman Catholic Archbishop of Armagh, the Primate of All Ireland, while his face is carved to resemble the Protestant Bishop of Dublin.

Statue of St Patrick at Slieve Patrick.

## CHAPTER 9:
# In Patrick's Footsteps – The Pilgrim Paths

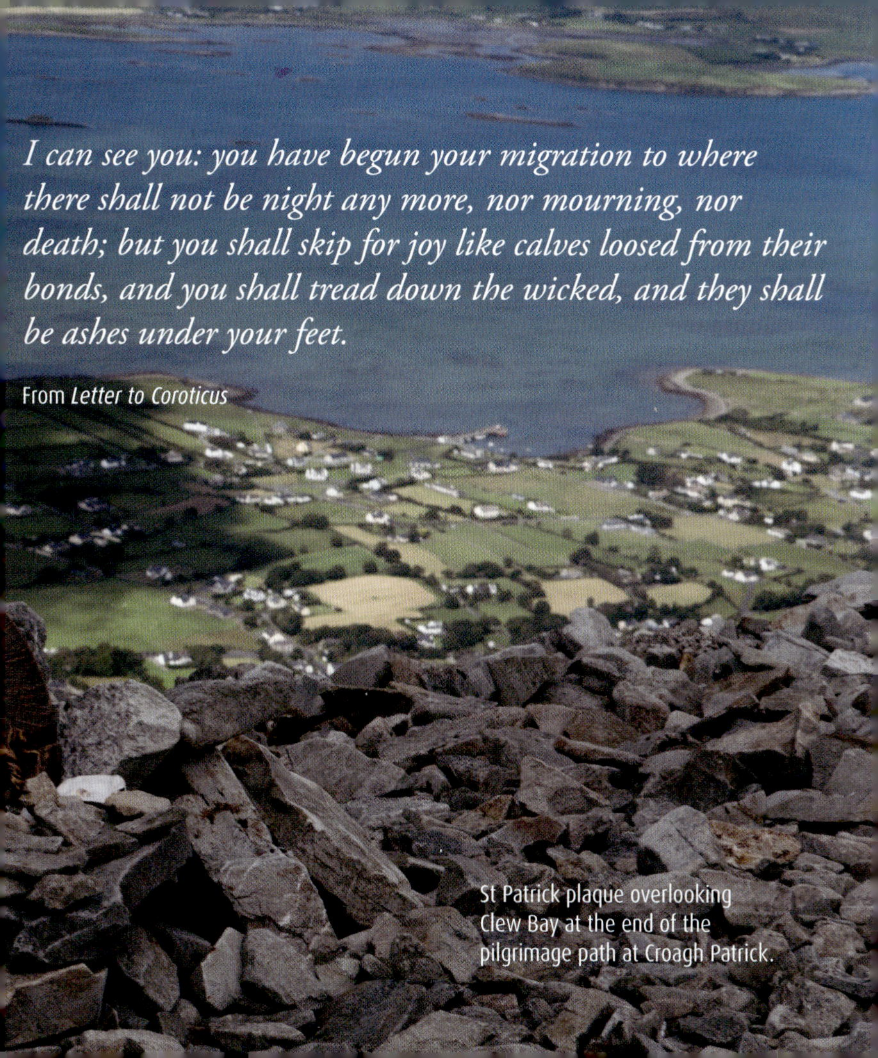

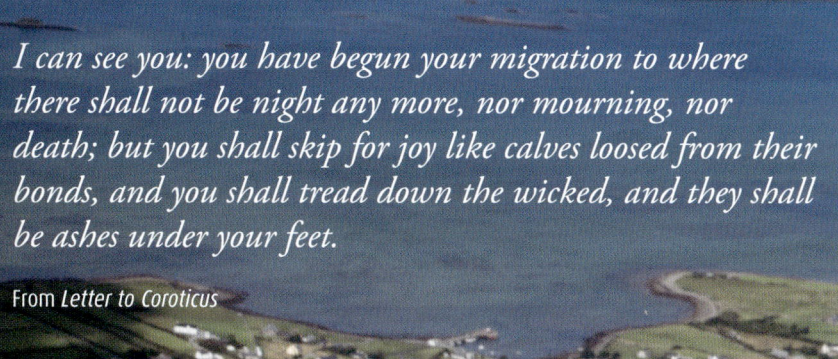

*I can see you: you have begun your migration to where there shall not be night any more, nor mourning, nor death; but you shall skip for joy like calves loosed from their bonds, and you shall tread down the wicked, and they shall be ashes under your feet.*

From *Letter to Coroticus*

St Patrick plaque overlooking Clew Bay at the end of the pilgrimage path at Croagh Patrick.

The key action of Patrick's work was walking. He was a preacher, on foot, covering miles as he made his way to speak to as many people as possible on the island of Ireland. Every day was a sort of pilgrimage for him as he walked and delivered the word of God. That action has been emulated by the faithful for centuries. The pilgrimage – a walk that has one or more than one holy place as its destination – is a feature of religions across the world. The pilgrim can undertake the pilgrimage for many different reasons – perhaps to pray for a particular outcome, or to atone for sinful behaviour, or to visit a particular sacred relic, or to give thanks for a happy outcome. Whatever the reason, it is a journey that takes the pilgrim away from all they know, in order to bring them closer to God.

There are pilgrim routes in Ireland dedicated to different saints, such as Brigid and Declan, but naturally St Patrick's paths are the best known. We have already encountered the small pilgrimages to the holy wells on his feast day, but there are also more demanding paths that will take you in Patrick's footsteps. Here, we will look at four routes that you can take: the most recent addition to the pilgrim paths; the two most famous pilgrimages that are long and deeply associated with St Patrick; and an age-old route that you may not have heard of before.

## St Patrick's Way: Armagh–Downpatrick

This is the newest addition to the pilgrim paths of St Patrick, and it takes the walker from his primary ecclesiastical site of Armagh to his beloved Downpatrick, on the Lecale peninsula. It opened in 2015 and covers a distance of 132km. That's a good six- or seven-day walk for an experienced walker, so it requires pre-planning if you want to tackle it in one go. Alternatively, you could pick sections and complete the walk over time, at your own pace.

The walk starts at Eamain Mhacha/Navan Fort – the prehistoric fort that was the ancient seat of the kings of Ulster. It was in use as a ceremonial site since 5500 BC. From there the path goes to Armagh, now a vibrant city with much to explore. There's a long section next, 33km, to get from Armagh to Scarva, a beautiful walk through countryside. Then it's another 20km on to Newry, where the walk is alongside the Newry Canal towpath – a nice, flat, scenic route. There are fourteen locks along the canal, which is the oldest canal in Ireland or Britain, in use since 1742. (It closed in the 1940s.) Next destination is the beautiful town of Rostrevor, about 15km from Newry. This brings you down to the sea and the town's stunning location in the shadow of Slieve Donard, the highest mountain in the Mournes range and in Northern Ireland. The path joins the Lecale Way as it travels through Murlough Nature Reserve and its rolling sand dunes, and into the town of Tyrella. Finally, there is a 16km walk from there to Downpatrick. This is hallowed ground in the story of Patrick – the site of Down cathedral and his alleged burial site. This is where the pilgrimage ends.

One of the lovely things about this pilgrim path is that you can collect a very special souvenir of your pilgrimage: the Pilgrim Walk Passport. This is available at the visitor information centres in the area. There is a booklet to guide you along the path, and it sets out the ten locations along the route where you can get your Passport stamped. When you bring the stamped Passport to the St Patrick Centre in Downpatrick, at the end of your very long trek, you will be presented with a certificate of achievement. This shows that you are a pilgrim of St Patrick and have walked the land where he lived and died.

## Lough Derg: the penance of Patrick

There are two pilgrimages that are famous the world over – one is Croagh Patrick in County Mayo, the other is Station Island on Lough Derg in County Donegal. This is where, the story goes, Patrick came in 445, alone, to do penance, pray and find spiritual communion with God. There are forty-six islands dotted around the Lough, but just two relate to the story of Patrick: Station

Island and Saint's Island. There was a traditional belief that Patrick founded a monastery on Saint's Island, appointing Dabheoc as the first abbot. What he found on Station Island is a whole other story – one that riveted the medieval period and created a devoted cult following.

Station Island has another, older name: Purgatorium Sancti Patricci – St Patrick's Purgatory. The earliest account of the story of Patrick on this island dates to 1152 and a treatise called De Purgatorio S. Patritii, written by Henry of Saltrey, a Benedictine monk. According to this, Patrick went to the island where he descended into a cave and there God showed him the torments of purgatory and hell:

Lough Derg.

*Our Lord Jesus Christ, visibly appearing to Saint Patrick, led him into a desert place, and there showed him a circular cave, dark inside, and at the same time said to him, whoever, armed with the true faith, and truly penitent, will enter that cave and remain in it for the space of a day and a night, will be purged from the sins of his whole life and moreover, passing through it, if his faith fail not he will witness not only the torments of the damned but also the joys of the blessed.*

The monk Saltrey then backed up this extraordinary story by adding the story of Oenus (Owen) Miles. This brave twelfth-century soldier-knight, who hailed from Ireland, had undertaken a pilgrimage to Lough Derg. An order of Augustinian monks had been established on the island in the twelfth century, and they oversaw Owen's 15-day fast and prayer rituals before leading him to the cave of Purgatory. He descended into the pit, and they locked the entrance behind him. For twenty-four hours Owen stayed alone in the cave, and in that time he described being assaulted and tempted and tested by all manner of spirits and demons. He witnessed the persecutions of hell, the pain and eternal suffering of those damned souls banished there. Owen kept repeating his call to God to save him: *'Jesus, as thou art full of might / Have mercy on me, sinful knight.'* He was granted mercy.

Owen was led to a bridge that crossed him over to the land where the souls destined for heaven were waiting peacefully and patiently. When the monks unlocked the door, Owen emerged from the cave a changed man. His sins had been cleansed, his soul purified, and his place in heaven was now assured. He had survived the rare and unique ordeal of descending into purgatory – and returning.

This account of St Patrick's Purgatory proved a sensational story, one that reverberated right around Europe. The idea of a descent into the torments of hell was utterly compelling – the ability to experience a world apart from this one, to test one's mettle against the powers of evil and emerge victorious, or, as the stories warned, not to emerge at all. It was sinister, it was dangerous and it was devilishly heroic – and the spirit of adventure seized many of those who heard the tale. Images began to circulate of this incredible place, such as that in the *Golden Legend* which shows a medieval pilgrim eagerly climbing into the cave, the blessings of the monks ringing in his ears. A good example of the effect and reach of this story is a fresco unearthed in the 1970s in Umbria. It was found in the Servite monastery of St Marco and dates to 1346. It vividly depicts St Patrick, in his bishop's regalia, extending his staff into the pit. The cave hosts the seven vices, each one attended by a tormenting devil. St Philip Benizi of Florence receives white-robed souls who are emerging from the cave, greeting them with olives branches and flowers. These are the virtuous ones, who will escape the fires of hell.

As the story spread, the pilgrims began to arrive in droves. St Patrick's Purgatory became one of the most famous sites in the world, hosting pilgrims from as far away as Switzerland, Hungary, Spain and Italy, eager to experience first-hand this otherworldly place. It became a focal point on maps of Ireland. The pilgrims wrote accounts of their strange experiences there, and a number of these have survived. St Patrick's Purgatory was the ultimate adventure, and many wanted to say they had been there – and survived to tell the tale. These pilgrims followed Owen's journey by typically spending fifteen days praying and fasting, before descending the steps down into the entrance to the cave. When the door clanged shut behind them, they were left in the dark for a twenty-four-hour vigil that would no doubt be an unforgettable experience: they might meet God … or the devil himself.

Those who wished to experience purgatory in this way were those who travelled from the Continent. Interestingly, the Irish pilgrims didn't view Lough Derg in the same way. For them, it was solely about penance and prayer, and they didn't seem to perform the 15-day fast and enter the cave. But for those who travelled to Ireland, it was the highlight and main attraction. The dramatic nature of the pilgrimage was pushed even further in the fourteenth century, when a new feature was added to the pre-descent ritual. Now, after two weeks of fasting and penitential prayer, the pilgrim received the Office of the Dead on the night before entering the cave. This was carried out in theatrical style: the pilgrim lay in a coffin, no doubt candlelight flickered dimly, and around him the Requiem Mass was intoned, including Psalm 114:

*The sorrows of death have compassed me: and the pains of hell have found me.*
*I have found tribulation, and sorrow: and I called on the name of our Lord.*

For the Church authorities in Rome, news of what was happening in Lough Derg was disturbing. Even worse were the reports of pilgrims being forced to pay to gain access to the island. Pope Alexander VI decided to put a stop to it and ordered the cave to be closed in 1497. But this was an ancient Irish site of pilgrimage, likely dating back to before Patrick's time, and it wasn't going to be easy to keep people away. In 1503 the archbishop of Armagh requested permission to reopen it – but this time it was kept as a local tradition, without the stream of foreign visitors with their money and their magical expectations. It became a site of penitential prayer once again. In 1632, during the Reformation, it was suppressed once more and everything on the island destroyed. The cave of St Patrick's Purgatory was never opened again, and was filled in in 1790, but there was no keeping the people away from this holy island.

From 1590, there were accounts of a three-day pilgrimage based on station prayers. If you wish to become part of this long tradition, this same pilgrimage can be carried out to this day. Every year in the pilgrimage season, which runs from 1 June to 15 August,

Sanctuary of St Patrick, Lough Derg, County Donegal.

more than 10,000 people visit Station Island on Lough Derg and perform one of the most challenging pilgrimages in the world. They undertake three days of fasting, walking and praying, with an all-night vigil as they repeat the nine stations and their 280 prayers. Many pilgrims do this barefoot, walking the pattern between the penitential beds.

The modern Station Island has accommodation for the pilgrims and an imposing basilica, which opened in 1931. Inside the basilica, we find once again the work of Harry Clarke – who we met in Chapter 8 – who created a series of 14 stained-glass windows showing the Stations of the Cross. The Clarke windows are a welcome blaze of light and colour within the grey, functional interior.

The pilgrimage at Lough Derg honours a long tradition of the island as a sacred or holy place. There may be no dramatic visions and demons any more, but it remains a truly important site for pilgrims. Some are devout, some are seeking a spiritual connection, some are taking time out to reconnect with themselves. All of them report that three days on Lough Derg is demanding but uniquely touching, and often reinvigorating. It is rare in our modern world to get time away from all distractions, time to reflect deeply, to be silent, to focus inwards rather than outwards, and this is what the trip to Station Island grants to the traveller. It seems safe to assume it is one part of his legacy of which Patrick would heartily approve.

## Croagh Patrick: Patrick's holy mountain

Now we come to the classic pilgrimage, probably the best-known Patrick pilgrimage of all – Croagh Patrick in County Mayo, standing 765m high with absolutely stunning views of Clew Bay and its fabled 365 drumlin islands far below – if the clouds don't spoil it. While the mountain is now firmly embedded in the Patrick story, there is archaeological evidence to suggest it was an important site for about five thousand years. There are Bronze Age cairns, for example, and the remains of a drystone oratory thought to date to the fifth century, *c.*430. As we saw earlier, this was a prime example of Patrick grafting the Christian tradition onto an existing pagan tradition. The mountain was already a place of ritual, now it is a place of Christian ritual and annual pilgrimage.

The first recorded reference to pilgrims at Croagh Patrick is given in the Annals for the year 1113. This notes that thirty pilgrims died when a terrific thunderstorm lashed the summit on St Patrick's Day. From then, it has been a hugely important annual pilgrimage route, with the pilgrimage being undertaken at night until 1973. There are walkers and pilgrims on the mountain all year, but the biggest day for pilgrims is Reek Sunday, which is the last Sunday in July. The mountain is known locally as 'The Reek', hence the name. On that day, around 25,000 people walk up to the summit, some of them barefoot in honour of the old tradition. It is a fantastic day out, especially when the sun shines, with a sense of community and camaraderie and common purpose. The pilgrims arm themselves with walking sticks bought or rented from the shop at the base of the mountain and they pray and encourage their way to the summit. It is a very special experience.

When they reach the summit, they can offer up a prayer in the church that was built there in 1905 by twelve local men. They used donkeys to transport the stone and cement required – an incredible feat by both man and beast when you consider it's a 4km vertical climb. The church was the first huge undertaking – the second was completed in 2024. This is the path, with steps, that threads its way from St Patrick's statue at the start of the climb right to the summit. It was a labour of love, sweat and dedication over three years by a local team of men, who went out in all weathers. In order to protect the habitat and make the mountain safe for walkers, they had to remove tonnes of rock and soil to make the 2m-wide path. Thanks to their Herculean efforts, there is less erosion and a safer path for pilgrims to ascend.

The church at the top of Croagh Patrick.

In the area around the holy mountain there is another ancient pilgrim path that wends its way from Ballintubber Abbey to Croagh Patrick and can still be followed to this day. This is the path of Tóchar Phádraig (St Patrick's Causeway), a 35km route through peaceful, beautiful countryside. It is thought to be the way of a processional path that stretched from Rathcroghan – the ancient capital of Connacht and seat of its kings and queens, most notably, Queen Medb – to Aughagower (Achadh Fhobhair, 'Field of the Springs'), site of Leaba Phádraig, ('St Patrick's bed'), where Patrick is said to have slept on his journey to the mountain and also where he is said to have founded a church – and finally to Croagh Patrick.

Today's pilgrim registers at Ballintubber Abbey to commence their pilgrimage. In doing so, they are echoing the ancient pilgrimage route to Croagh Patrick, which was approached from the east. This is a historic and spiritual landscape, with holy wells, pillar stones, a round tower and a sacred tree along the route. One of the oldest and most interesting finds is the Boheh Stone, also known as St Patrick's Chair, which is about 6km from Westport. This large boulder is pitted with cup and ring marks – otherwise known as petroglyphs. These prehistoric rock carvings would have been made *c.*3800 BC. It is quite an experience to run your fingers through and around these markings, knowing they were carved by other hands thousands of years ago.

In the 1980s/1990s, a local researcher, Gerry Bracken, was engaged in cataloguing the many monuments in the Westport area when he made an astonishing discovery. If you are standing at the Boheh Stone on 18 and on 24 August as evening falls, you can watch the sun rolling down the side of Croagh Patrick. The path of the setting sun matches the angle of the mountain's northern slope and so it looks like the sun rolls gently down the side and away off to its resting place. The Boheh Stone has now become a pilgrimage in its own right as local people gather to witness this incredible phenomenon.

## Sacred *Mám Éan*

Finally, there is a pilgrim path that is not so well known, but is an unforgettable place to visit. You'll need sturdy walking boots for this one as you are walking in the Maumturk mountains to find this ancient site hidden away in their rocky folds. This site has been a place of pilgrimage for centuries, originally linked to Lughnasa, the Celtic harvest festival on 1 August. Then the story of Patrick took over and Mám Éan became associated with his work. The legend goes that when Patrick came here, the locals weren't too interested in hearing the word of God and threw stones at him. Patrick flung his staff at them, which turned into a serpent and scattered the people, leaving them awestruck. His point was made.

After that, Patrick built a church and a stone altar to consecrate the site and blessed a well, making it Tobar Phádraig or St Patrick's Holy Well. These are still here, along with stones to represent the Stations of the Cross. Most visitors describe it as a strange sort of place – remote and starkly beautiful. If you make the 1.3km hike up to the chapel, you will also find one of the most affecting statues of St Patrick. It was sculpted by Cliodhna Cussen in 1986 and now stands near the chapel. It shows a contemplative Patrick, a sheep at his feet, his chin resting on his staff, seemingly lost in prayer. Its hunched, stoic form matches the atmosphere of this hidden-away place.

A view across the remote Maumturk Mountains in the Connemara region of County Galway.

Mám Éan – the Pass of the Birds – is still visited by pilgrims on three important feast days: St Patrick's Day, Good Friday and Reek Sunday. The water of the holy well is said to cure ailments, and you can also tie a rag to the nearby hawthorn tree to ask for a blessing. It is a place that feels deeply old and spiritual, rooted in Ireland's past, and a memorable place to echo the footsteps of St Patrick.

## Did you know?

✤ In the basilica on Station Island, on its plain, simple altar stands a large cross that is unusual and haunting. This is the work of renowned sculptor Imogen Stuart (1927–2024), who based it on a tragedy that befell a boat of pilgrims. On 12 July 1795, 93 pilgrims and crew were making their way across the waters of the lough on the 11 a.m. ferry when the boat sprung a leak. The panic-stricken passengers scrambled to escape, but to no avail. Reports record that between 70 and 90 people met their death in the lough that day. One of those who died was Mary O'Donnell. When her body was recovered, her hand was tightly gripping a small wooden penal cross, dated 1722. Stuart created her cross based on this little symbol of despair and hope.

✤ Ireland has a wealth of beautiful ways and paths, and some of these have now been gathered together under the aegis of a pilgrim passport. There is an 'Irish Camino' that can be undertaken and that ends at Ballintubber Abbey. If your passport has stamps from five ancient pilgrim routes, you will receive a pilgrim certificate at the Abbey to mark your pilgrimage (see www.pilgrimpath.ie). In 2025, to mark the Jubilee Year, a new pilgrim passport was created for those completing a pilgrimage to Lough Derg, Knock Shrine and Croagh Patrick (see www.pilgrimpassport.ie). And for those with even wider horizons, there is a Celtic Camino that is linked to the Camino de Santiago (the Way of St James). This is defined by the Camino Society of Ireland as a 25km pilgrimage completed in Ireland combined with the 75km pilgrimage from A Coruña to Santiago. Once you reach the cathedral in Santiago, your passport will receive its final completion stamp – and you will have walked in the footsteps of Irish medieval pilgrims since the twelfth century.

✥ Finally, the Mámean Pilgrimage Trail, which is part of the Western Way, is also now part of the International Appalachian Trail. When you traverse the mountainous way at Mám Éan, you are walking on rocks that are 450 million years old and geologically link Ireland with North America. That's the beauty of every pilgrimage – it is a walk through history.

*CHAPTER 10:*
# Visiting Patrick's Ireland

*… if I have accomplished or brought to light any small part of God's purpose, none shall ever assert that the credit is due to my own uneducated self, but regard it rather as a true fact to be firmly believed that it was all the gift of God.*

From *Confession*

A panoramic view of Croagh Patrick mountain.

There are many, many places that echo with Patrick's footsteps and his legends across the island of Ireland, but we can only visit a small selection here. This, then, is a select list, three from each province – so a holy dozen of very beautiful and very fascinating sites. These are all places you can visit when in Ireland to explore the story of St Patrick.

## ULSTER

## Armagh and its cathedrals

The city of Armagh is a beautiful and interesting place to explore, not least because it is unique in having two cathedrals, both dedicated to the one saint. The Cathedral Church of St Patrick, Armagh, is an Anglican church located on the hill where Patrick was said to have founded his first church in AD445. It looks across at the hill of Druim Saileach, where stands the imposing St Patrick's Cathedral, the Roman Catholic church. Together, they embody the broad Christian heritage handed down by St Patrick, embracing both faiths equally.

St Patrick's Cathedral has two soaring spires, reaching 63m high, and is designed in the Gothic style. Stepping inside, you meet a breathtaking interior, high and bright, wreathed with stained-glass windows, detailed mosaics and a high altar made of fine Italian marble. It is still and tranquil, inviting the visitor to take a seat and reflect. There is also a museum, with many artefacts and relics. The glorious windows show scenes from the life of St Patrick, among other saints, including his dream of Ireland, receiving his mission from Pope Celestine and his death at Saul.

The Cathedral of St Patrick is, by contrast, a more austere, simpler church, both inside and out, but it shares the same prayerful stillness as its Catholic counterpart. Its stained-glass windows commemorate the story of Patrick saving the life of a fawn at this spot. The building has been ruined and rebuilt throughout its history, and now is a beautiful holy space that preserves the records and books of Armagh's history. It also preserves the final resting place of Brian Boru, one of Ireland's most celebrated kings, who was struck down at the Battle of Clontarf in 1014 while he was at prayer. In the Cathedral's walled gardens, there is a striking statue of Brian Boru by sculptor Rory Breslin.

Armagh always advanced its primacy on the basis of its special connection with St Patrick and his desire for it to be the first among all the ecclesiastical centres on the island of Ireland. It has successfully defended that status and remains the seat of the primate of All Ireland in both the Roman Catholic and Church of

Ireland traditions. The archbishops of Armagh, both RC and CoI, are the most senior churchmen on the island to this day.

## Slemish, County Antrim

As we know from the early life of Patrick, Slemish is the place where it is believed he was brought as a 16-year-old slave to work as a shepherd. The hill rises, humpbacked, above the neatly stone-walled fieldscape of County Antrim. It stands only 437m high, but as it's the only high point, it has sweeping views on all sides. Slemish is the core of an ancient volcano, so it would have once been magma filling a crater. When the magma cooled, this lump of dolerite remained, and was then weathered and eroded into its current shape. For Patrick, his rocky, windswept open-air 'prison' would have afforded him very little shelter.

Slemish Mountain.

Slemish can be visited and climbed all year round, but it also a place of pilgrimage on St Patrick's Day. Large crowds gather and walk together to the summit in honour of Patrick. The nearby village of Broughshane is beautifully and proudly kept, earning its title of the 'Garden Village of Ulster'. It is a good spot to stop and explore on the way to or from an encounter with Slemish and Patrick's six years as a slave, at the spot where he found God and changed the path of his life forever.

## Downpatrick, County Down

We have already encountered the town of Downpatrick and the Cathedral Church of the Holy Trinity, known as Down Cathedral and said to be final resting place of St Patrick, St Brigid and St Colmcille. Downpatrick is a richly historic town surrounded by lush countryside and one of the most important sites when following in the footsteps of Patrick. You can do this very easily by following the historic walking tour of Downpatrick, a self-guided walk that takes you to all of the key sites.

The trail starts at the St Patrick Centre, with its unique exhibition. It takes you to Down Cathedral, up on the Hill of Down, with fine views across the town. The cathedral and the gravestone of Patrick are huge attractions. You'll also visit Down County Museum, located in the eighteenth-century Down

County gaol. An interesting spot on the trail is Inch Abbey, which was established by John de Courcy – who made the 'miraculous' discovery of the saints' bones. This was the monastery to which he brought Jocelin of Furness, to write his famous *Life of Patrick*. (It is also, for *Game of Thrones* fans, the filming location for Robb Stark's camp.)

The walking tour ends at Inch Abbey, but that is not the end of the places worth visiting. Struell Wells, which we visited in Chapter 10, lies just 2.4km from Downpatrick – a place with a special, spiritual energy and, the story has it, a place once visited by Patrick himself. Three kilometres outside Downpatrick is the simple church of Saul, said to be the site of Patrick's very first church on the island. And there is also Raholp Church, 4.8km away from Downpatrick and just ruins now, but dedicated to St Tassach, who is said to have administered the Last Rites to St Patrick as he lay dying in Saul, his 'homeplace' in Ireland.

## MUNSTER

### St Patrick's Well, Clonmel

There is a story told in the tenth-century *Life of St Declan* that St Patrick was on his way to Cashel when he stopped here, in Clonmel, and visited with his friend, St Declan. The marker of

*Visiting Patrick's Ireland*

this legendary visit is this holy well, which is one of the largest in Ireland. It is a very beautiful and peaceful spot, featuring a large pool with a Celtic-style cross at its centre, made of sandstone. This cross is reckoned to be eighth-century, which would make it the oldest feature of the holy well. It was moved to its current position in the 1960s during renovation works.

There is a stone church beside the lake, roofless now and dating to the fifteenth/sixteenth century. Inside you can see an altar tomb for the White family. There is a flight of stone steps leading down to the site, at the end of which the visitor is greeted by a large statue of St Patrick. The well, now encircled by a stone wall, is a natural well, with the water rising up from below-ground. The water enters the well through two carved stone water spouts, and then exits into a large, shallow pool and then out to join a tributary of the River Suir.

St Patrick's Well, Clonmel.

It has long been held that the water has the power to cure ailments, particularly sore lips and eyes. There are some wonderful stories about it in the National Folklore Collection (see www.duchas.ie). One recollection from 1938 tells us: *'There is a well outside Clonmel and it is call St. Patrick's well. If a person prays to St. Patrick every day he will be healed of any blemish he may have. One time a boy and had to use crutches. Every day he used to go to St. Patrick's well to pray. One day he thought he would try to walk without the crutches and he walked.'* To this day, the well is a place of pilgrimage for those who wish to receive a blessing from St Patrick or a cure from its blessed waters.

## Rock of Cashel – St Patrick's Rock

Following the road from Clonmel *c.*31km, you will find one of the most breathtaking sites on the island: the Rock of Cashel. We already heard the story of how Patrick converted Óengus, the King of Munster, and baptised him in a public ceremony at the Rock (page 131). This story cemented the saint's association with Cashel, the alternative name for which became St Patrick's Rock, or Carraig Phádraig. From this sprang two legends: one, that the devil had taken up residence in a cave on Devil's Bit Mountain and Patrick threw him from there with such force, a chunk of the

Rock of Cashel castle.

mountain was hurled as far as Cashel; the other, that the devil fought back with a vengeance and he and Patrick had an epic battle – but when the devil realised he couldn't best the saint, he exploded the mountain to escape and a chunk of it landed in Cashel.

When you visit, you can see why people told tales about the origin of this dramatic limestone outcrop of rock that rises 61m above the surrounding landscape. It is as imposing as it is impressive, rearing up out of the landscape, its remarkable buildings marking the skyline. It holds the remains of a number of awesome monuments, including a round tower, a high cross, a Romanesque chapel, an abbey, a Gothic cathedral and the wonderfully sculpted Hall of the Vicars Choral. Cormac's Chapel houses the only surviving Romanesque frescoes in Ireland.

Its history stretches back before Patrick, but it remained a royal stronghold until the eleventh century. In 1101, King Muirchertach O'Brien gave the Rock into the care of the Church, and from then on it was an ecclesiastical powerhouse. As well as having a role in religious politics over the centuries, it also remained a sacred site of pilgrimage and prayer. In 2024, more than 365,000 people visited the Rock, drawn by its beauty, its unique energy and its close ties to the story of St Patrick.

# St Patrick's Holy Well, Rossalia, County Clare

This simple well is very different from the well at Clonmel, its opposite in size and setting, albeit its equal in holiness. It is a small, hidden-away well, tucked into the stony contours of the Burren on Abbey Hill, which is used for the winter grazing of cattle. It is a naturally occurring spring beside a public track, and there is just a small ivory statue to let you know that you have located it successfully. When you do find it, you'll be rewarded with gorgeous views sweeping across Galway Bay.

This well has been encircled by a drystone structure, with the little statue perched into the cliff above. It is located not far from the busy tourist towns of Ballyvaughan and Kinvarra, but it seems that it is no longer much visited. There is a hawthorn tree about 20 metres away with ribbons on its branches, so there must be some pilgrims still making their way here. It was long believed that its clear spring waters had curative properties. An entry in the Folklore Collection for 1937 records that *'People who were suffering from pain in their limbs visited the well for the cure. They washed the affected part with the holy water.'*

The well is dedicated to St Patrick, therefore his feast day remains the important day for pilgrimage. There is also a memorial stone about 10m down the slope from the well, inscribed with the names 'John Cornym' and 'Mary M Nemara' and a date that appears to read '1765'. This is a humble, quiet, out-of-the-way site, but any traveller through this landscape would be happy to stumble upon this little sacred space and send up a prayer to Patrick.

## CONNACHT

## Downpatrick Head, County Mayo

There are debates around whether Patrick ever did set foot as far south as Munster, but it seems to be a fact that he did go to Connacht – primarily because he himself mentions Foclut, in Mayo, in his *Confession*. There are many sites in Mayo associated with the saint, but perhaps the most spectacular is Downpatrick Head, on the wild Atlantic coast. It lies between the village of

St Patrick statue, Downpatrick Head, County Mayo.

Ballycastle and the Céide Fields, one of the oldest Stone Age farming sites in the world and a must-visit if you are in the area. Just 14km away you'll reach Downpatrick Head, with its wide vista of the Atlantic and its stories of Patrick.

There is a statue of Patrick on the headland, and although it is said that he founded a church here, the association with the saint is mainly that of legend and folklore. Standing on the headland, you look out on the Dún Briste sea stack and the group of rocky islands known as the Stags of Broadhaven. It is a truly stunning vista, complete with the sky-weavings of puffins, kittiwakes, and cormorants. Dún Briste is a 50m high sea stack, jutting out of the waves 80m from the shore. The official story is that it separated from the mainland in 1393 during a violent storm, but the legend is that Patrick faced off with the druid Crom Dubh here, and the druid fell back to his fort at the edge of the headland, whereupon Patrick struck his mighty staff into the ground, shearing the fort and the land on which it stood off from the rest of the island. Crom Dubh was trapped inside his 'broken fort' – Dún Briste in Irish.

There is another interesting feature at Downpatrick, and it also comes with its own Patrick legend. Poll na Seantainne – the Hole of the Old Fire – is a huge and deep blowhole. The same legend says that Crom Dubh started the fight by trying to throw the saint into a fire he conjured, but Patrick used his staff to scratch a cross onto a stone, threw the stone into the druid's fire, and the ground beneath collapsed down into the sea, forming the blowhole. Since 2014, the feature has become the centre of an installation called The Crossing, designed by architecture students from the Catholic University of America. This has created a viewing point from which you can look down into the wild sea far below.

## Kilgeever Abbey, County Mayo

The Clew Bay Heritage Trail sets out 21 archaeological sites from Westport to Louisburgh and on to Granuaile's castle on Clare Island. One of those sites is Kilgeever Abbey. It is situated 3km outside Louisburgh, a small town that's often overlooked but has an interesting history, a vibrant local community, and a hinterland rich in archaeology and stunning, empty beaches.

The site at Kilgeever has the ruins of a medieval church, a graveyard and a holy well with stations. It is a quiet, tranquil place where St Patrick is said to have come after his forty nights up on Croagh Patrick and where he is said to have a built a church. That story created a pilgrimage route linking Kilgeever with Croagh Patrick. In times gone by, locals walked up Croagh Patrick on Reek Sunday, then completed the pilgrimage by walking on to

Kilgeever and doing the stations there. This was a very specific pattern of circuits and prayers, in sets of seven. Some collected seven stones from the holy well at the start and dropped one stone at the completion of each circuit, to keep count. This was a common ritual at many sites.

The central monument of the devotions here is the holy well in the graveyard. This is known locally as Tobar Rí an Dhomhnaigh – Our Lord's Well of the Sabbath. It is a small well, topped by stone and a stone cross, and the pilgrims kneel at it to recite their prayers. Kilgeever is a site and a pilgrimage that has changed very little over the years and therefore still retains a spiritual atmosphere, set apart from the busy world. It is a tranquil place to spend some time as you trace Patrick's story across Mayo.

## Coney Island, Sligo

If your first thought when hearing 'Coney Island' is Long Island, New York, you'll be intrigued to learn that the more famous Coney Island is said to have taken its name from this much lesser-known Irish placename. Apparently, the captain of the *Arethusa*, a merchant ship that plied its trade between Sligo and New York, was taken by the fact that Sligo's Coney Island was named because of a proliferation of rabbits (*coinín* – rabbit) – just as rabbits were populating his NY Coney Island at a fierce rate. So he brought the name home and that's how his homeplace got its name. (Although the Dutch will tell you it comes from *konijn,* the Dutch word for rabbit.)

Sligo's Coney Island lies in Sligo Bay, one of three islands between Rosses Point and Strandhill. It's just 2.4km x 1.2km and while it's accessible by boat from Rosses Point, it is only accessible via Cummeen Strand when the tide is out. When the tide retreats, the strand and its 14 stone pillars are exposed, allowing you to make your way the 5km across the causeway. But knowledge of the tide times is absolutely crucial if you don't want to get stranded out there.

That said, you'd be stranded in a pure haven of beauty and quiet. The legend says that St Patrick came out to the island for prayer and reflection, and that the spot he chose is the rock now known as St Patrick's Wishing Chair. On his feast day, a person can sit on the stone and make a single wish and it may be granted.

Coney Island.

There is also a holy well dedicated to St Patrick out on the island and locals have plenty of folklore tales about his time spent there.

When you return across the strand, you can also visit Kilaspugbrone Church in nearby Strandhill. This is where St Patrick was visiting when he lost a tooth. He gave his tooth to Bishop Brón, who was one of his disciples and after whom Kilaspugbrone is named – the Church of Bishop Brón. The Bishop enshrined the precious tooth in the church and it was passed down through the generations. In 1376 a silver and gold shrine was crafted to hold the saint's relic – and this is the Shrine of the Tooth that is still on display to this day, now in the National Museum in Dublin (see page 165).

## LEINSTER

## St Patrick's Cathedral, Dublin

The Gothic splendour of Dublin's St Patrick's Cathedral dominates the skyline of the old Liberties area of the city. It is built on the alleged site of a holy well that was used by Patrick to baptise his converts in the fifth century. Whatever church was on the site in the twelfth century, it was enlarged in 1191 by John Cumin, the first Anglo-Norman archbishop of Dublin. In the 1200s, work began on the fine cathedral we see today, with its vaulted roofs, buttresses and spires. It has been modified many times since then, with one particularly beautiful addition being the Lady Chapel, which in 1665 was handed over to the Huguenots as their place of worship and renamed L'Eglise Française de St Patrick.

When works were being carried out in 1901 to create St Patrick's Park next to the cathedral, the workmen found a stone said to mark the location of Patrick's holy well. This is now on display. It is one among a very many historic artefacts to be explored in the cathedral. This is also the final resting place of Dean Jonathan Swift, author of *Gulliver's Travels*; he is buried there alongside his 'beloved friend', Esther Johnson. Another interesting feature is the banners of the Knights of St Patrick, which hang over the choir stalls, commemorating the now-defunct order established in 1783 by King George III as the Most Illustrious Order of St Patrick.

One of the more eccentric historic artefacts is the Door of Reconciliation. This is a stout medieval door with a hole right through it. In the fifteenth century, the Butlers and FitzGeralds were engaged in a bloody pitched battle nearby and the Butlers ran and hid in the cathedral, locking the door of the Chapter House behind them. The FitzGeralds came after in hot pursuit. Gerald FitzGerald ordered them to come out and make peace, but the Butlers were understandably nervous of being slaughtered to a man. The solution? A hole was cut in the door, Gerald stuck his arm through – taking a gamble it wouldn't be lopped off – and they shook on it. According to tradition, this is where the phrase 'to chance your arm' comes from.

## The Hills of Slane and Tara, County Meath

You can visit the sites of one of the most famous Patrick stories – the story of how he lit the paschal fire on the Hill of Slane so that the High King in Tara could see it and know that a new order had arrived on the island (see page 112). The two hills lie c.21km distant, with the one visible from the other. Both are worth visiting on a tour of the Boyne Valley.

The Hill of Slane is the reputed burial place of Sláine mac Dela, the first high king of Ireland and one of the Fir Bolg – in legend these were the kings of Ireland for a time before being ousted by the Tuatha Dé

The Door of Reconcilliation, St Patrick's Cathedral.

Danann. The hill is just 4km from the World Heritage Property of Brú na Bóinne, which encompasses the ancient sites of Newgrange, Knowth and Dowth – these prehistoric passage tombs, built *c.*3200BC, are often the reason visitors make their way to County Meath in the first place. If you push on to Slane, you'll find a hilltop monument that is steeped in history and, on a clear day, fine views across the county.

The hill was the site of a monastery founded by St Erc in the sixth century. He was bishop of Slane and was consecrated by St Patrick. The large graveyard enclosure has a holy well, now dried up, that is dedicated to St Patrick. There is also the sixteenth-century St Patrick's parish church and a tall Gothic tower. Beyond the walls of the enclosure are the remains of a college founded in 1512 by Sir Christopher Fleming. On its stone remains you can find carvings of Tudor roses and the coat-of-arms of the king of England and France.

The Hill of Tara commands a panoramic view that takes in at least seven counties on a good day and includes the historic monument of Loughcrew Cairns, the Hill of Slane and Trim Castle. It is one of the most important archaeological sites of ancient Ireland, in use since the Stone Age, when a passage tomb was built. In the Iron Age (600BC–AD400) it became a key ceremonial site as the seat of the high king of Ireland. There were five ancient royal roads *(slíghe)* in Ireland, and they all led to Tara: Slige Midluachra ran north from Tara to Eamain Mhacha; Slige Mhór ran from Tara to Esker Riada; Slige Cualann ran from Tara to County Wicklow; Slige Dála ran southwest, to Kilkenny; Slige Asail ran to Lough Owel. The Hill of Tara was thus the centre of ceremony and trade.

On top of the hill, you have to use your imagination to picture Tara in its royal heyday because the remains are largely earthworks – huge ditches and banks rolling across the land. But there is a particular energy at Tara that marks it out as special place. According to legend, it was to here the young slave Patrick was brought and held in the Mound of the Hostages – an ancient passage tomb. That wasn't Patrick's only experience of Tara. He returned as a preacher, taking on Tara's mighty druids, so the story goes, and beating them with his divine miracles. There are stories and there are facts about Tara, and you will hear them both on a guided tour of the hill, which is the best way to uncover the full and intriguing history of the hill. (Note that guided tours from the visitor centre are available from May to September only.)

## The Hill of Uisneach

Heading into County Westmeath, there is another hill that is wreathed in stories stretching back through time. Uisneach is known as the centre, and spiritual centre, of the island of Ireland. Its importance throughout history can be told from the remains of a ring fort, circular enclosures, ancient roads and cairns. There is also a spring known as St Patrick's Well. In the *Tripartite Life,* we are told that Patrick came to Uisneach in the fifth century because he wished to found a monastery on the hill. However, he was run off by the O'Neill clan. In return, Patrick set a curse on their heads, angrily declaring that the stones of Uisneach would never be of any use for any purpose, not building, not heating, not washing.

St Patrick may not have settled the hill for Christianity, but he is still associated with the site. At the summit there is a Neolithic tomb and it is called to this day St Patrick's Bed. From here, there are stunning views across the largely flat landscape of the central plains. One tradition has it that this was used as a Mass rock in penal times. There is not much to see there today, but geophysical surveys have peeled back the layers and shown that St Patrick's Bed was once encircled by a 25m diameter enclosure.

There is another very interesting rock up here, and it too was once within a ring-barrow enclosure. This is a misshapen limestone glacial erratic that stands almost 6m high and 5m wide. It is called

*Ail na Mireann* – the Stone of the Divisions – and is said to have been a territory marker, dividing the ancient provinces.

## Did you know?

✥ The truth about the well where St Patrick baptised converts in fifth-century Dublin might be a well-kept secret. Above, you read about St Patrick's Cathedral being the site of his baptisms, but there is another, little-known story that disputes this. At one time, the street signs on Nassau Street read: Sráid Thobar Phádraig / Nassau Street. The English name referred to the son of Lord Molesworth, Richard Nassau Molesworth, whereas the Irish name meant: St Patrick's Well Lane. This refers to a hidden holy well on the grounds of Trinity College. Near the Provost's House Stables there is a well-house that leads down and under Nassau Street. Within, there is a redbrick Georgian vaulted well with steps leading down to an oval basin. In 1729 the well ran dry, although nobody could say why, but today it is once again filled with water. This well is a protected structure, locked and inaccessible, but it lies there still, St Patrick's well, a quiet testament to an alternative history of Patrick's baptisms in Dublin.

✥ St Patrick's Hall in Dublin Castle is a sumptuous state room, decorated in rich blue and gold, where the Irish president is inaugurated for his or her seven-year term of office. Originally the castle ballroom, it was also the meeting place of the Knights of St Patrick, and the order's flags are still hanging on the walls. On the ceiling are three canvas paintings by Italian artist Vincenzo Waldré, one of which depicts St Patrick lighting the paschal fire at the Hill of Slane. Waldré completed these beautiful paintings between 1788 and 1802. Dublin Castle describes this as *'the most important painted ceiling to survive in Ireland from the eighteenth century'*.

## Myth vs fact

✤ We have seen that the story of St Patrick is a glorious mix of poignant fact and powerful fiction, and that sometimes it can be difficult to separate the two. If you wish to explore the historical evidence and associated relics, you can visit the National Museum of Ireland on Kildare Street in Dublin. Here, you can see St Patrick's bell and shrine and the Shrine of the Tooth. The ninth-century Book of Armagh is held in the Old Library in Trinity College Dublin, where you can view the 1,200-year-old Book of Kells as part of the immersive Book of Kells Experience (www.visittrinity.ie).

The ceiling of St Patrick's Hall, Dublin Castle, by Valdrè, Vincenzo, 1740–1814.

*CHAPTER 11:*
# The Greening of the Irish – St Patrick's Day in Ireland

*Lá Fhéile Pádraig sona duit!* –
Happy St Patrick's Day to you!

The evolution of St Patrick's feast day over the past four hundred years is a tale of Ireland itself, of how it has come of age as a hard-won republic. Patrick died on 17 March and in the early 1600s the Church recognised this date as his official feast day, making it a holy day to be observed by Catholics. It is a mark of the saint's life's work that his feast day is also observed by the Church of Ireland, the Eastern Orthodox Church and the Lutheran Church. That is pretty impressive for a saint who has never been canonised!

What started out as a holy day for pilgrimage and prayer became, over the centuries, a celebration of Irish heritage, history and identity as St Patrick and his legendary shamrock became the worldwide symbols of Ireland and Irishness. This dates right back to the seventeenth century, when a traveller from England, Thomas Dineley, observed the feast day in the 1680s and disparaged the behaviour he witnessed: *'The Irish of all stations and conditions wear crosses in their hats, some of pins, some of green ribbon, and the vulgar superstitiously wear shamrogues, 3-leaved grass, which they likewise eat (they say) to cause a sweet breath.'* Crosses, green and shamrocks – the key elements were all in place hundreds of years ago.

## 'This frightful exhibition'

We have already heard about the holy wells and the pilgrimages – both were the original ways for Irish communities across the island to honour St Patrick on 17 March every year. People would come together to walk the stations at the well, or to walk up Croagh Patrick or other holy places. This was the religious part of the day. But what followed was often not very holy at all.

One of the reasons for the long-lasting popularity of St Patrick's Day was that it fell in Lent – and it was treated as a day off. Lent lasted forty days and forty nights, matching the time Jesus spent in the desert. It was a time of fasting, reflection and prayer to ready the body and soul for the resurrection on Easter Sunday. But in the middle of all that came St Patrick's Day, with its God-given opportunity to take a break from being good. In 1726, Caleb Threlkeld – the writer who first gave us the link between shamrocks and St Patrick (see page 146) – noted of the Irish that *'when they wet their* Seamar-oge, *they often commit excess in liquor, which is not a right keeping of a day to the Lord; error generally leading to debauchery.'*

The giddy combination of a special day, permission to break the rules and gathering together to celebrate led to a sense of freedom that could spill over into drunkenness and, if Threlkeld is to be believed, debauchery. It wasn't what the Church had in mind when it honoured the country's patron saint with a feast day. The words of the Catholic archbishop of Cashel c.1840 on this matter were thunderous: *'It is become such a scene of drunkenness and quarrelling and of other most abominable vice, that religion herself is brought into disrepute nay mocked and ridiculed: intemperance and immorality are encouraged.'*

It seems to have been an issue that afflicted even the holy mountain itself. An 1842 description of the Croagh Patrick pilgrimage, recorded by William Makepeace Thackeray in his *Irish Sketch Book,* contains almost as much outrage as the Archbishop mustered – and this for both the religious aspect and the frivolous aspect. The author had it from a very reliable source that the barefoot pilgrims came *'… away from this frightful exhibition suffering severe pain, wounded and bleeding in the knees and feet and some of the women shrieking with the pain of their wounds. Fancy thousands of these bent upon their work and priests standing by to encourage them! For shame. For shame …'* And then after this:

> *The pleasures of the poor people – for after the business on the mountain came the dancing and love making at its foot – were woefully spoiled by the rain which rendered dancing on the grass impossible: nor were the tents big enough for that exercise.*

*The Greening of the Irish – St Patrick's Day in Ireland*

*The 16th, 17th (St Patrick's Day), and 18th March*
by Erskine Nicol, 1825-1904, National Gallery of Ireland.

*Indeed the whole sight was as dismal and half savage a one as I have seen … Men and women were crowded in these rude tents, huddled together and disappearing in the darkness.*

## The homesick Irish

Ireland has been an island of emigration for a long time. From the seventeenth century, people left to escape poverty or religious persecution. In the 1700s large numbers of Presbyterians emigrated from Ulster to America. At this time, Catholics were less likely to emigrate, but there was always a constant trickle of leavers. They didn't forget where they came from. In Boston, the Charitable Irish Society was founded on 17 March 1737, in recognition of St Patrick. The first members were *'twenty-six men of Ulster birth and ancestry'* and their purpose was to provide relief to Irish people in need and to promote the interests of Irish people.

Similarly, New York had a sizeable Irish-born population by the eighteenth century. This led to the very first St Patrick's Day parade on record, which seems to have come about by glorious accident. In 1762, the annual St Patrick's Day breakfast was being held at a tavern on Lower Broadway and some of the Irish military men heading to it took a whim to march there behind their army band, banners flying. It was a lighthearted, high-spirited moment and people passing by stopped to enjoy it. And that, it seems, is how the parade started. It caught on around the States and quickly became an anticipated part of the day.

The years of the Great Famine (1845–1852) saw Irish people

leave the island in huge numbers. The statistics are bleakly familiar: between 1845 and 1855, around 1.1 million died and around 1.5 million were forced to leave. A great many took the boat to America. They brought their language and customs with them, including their devotion to St Patrick. As with all emigrants, the emblems of home became even more significant, ever more tightly held, because they were the means by which to stay close to what was so far away.

The marking of 17 March took on a new meaning in the new places. The Friendly Societies and the growing Irish communities made St Patrick's Day more than a feast day – it was how they honoured their heritage and beliefs even as they worked hard to become part of their new country. And this is how Ireland ended up lagging behind in terms of celebrating the day. It was the Irish communities in America who started us on the path to the St Patrick's Day we are used to now. The idea of colourful, musical parades was sent back to us across the water – it wasn't created here in Ireland.

But what they did share, the Irish in America and Ireland, was a growing sense of Irishness. During the eighteenth and nineteenth centuries there was a growing restlessness under British rule, a growing demand for Irish freedom, and the traditions of St Patrick and the wearing of green and the shamrock became fused with that

1874 print of a St Patrick's Day parade in America.

sense of patriotism and nationhood. Now, the day and its customs became a sort of rebellion, a statement of intent. Slowly St Patrick's Day became a day to be unapologetically Irish, to embrace those roots and proclaim them, after generations of being held up as 'lesser than'. As in America, it became so much more than drink and divine intercession.

## If you're Irish ...

In 1903, the Bank Holiday Act (Ireland) was passed at Westminster Parliament and St Patrick's Day became a bank holiday. This gave official recognition to Patrick's status as patron saint and apostle of Ireland. In Waterford, it was decided to mark the new holiday with a procession through the city. There were marching bands, the mayor and a festive atmosphere. Waterford had just become the site of the very first St Patrick's parade in Ireland.

The first decades of the twentieth century saw Ireland move towards and finally achieve Independence in 1922, as the Irish Free State with 26 counties. Nine years later – and a full 169 years after New York – Ireland held its first official St Patrick's Day parade in 1931, in Dublin. It was a no-drinking event as the sale of alcohol on St Patrick's Day was banned from 1927 to 1961. The Catholic archbishop of Cashel would have no doubt approved!

From then on, the parade tradition grew year on year and now forms the centrepiece of the day right across the island. All of the other customs have been worked around this big event – whether it's the local town parade or the extravaganza of Dublin's St Patrick's Festival. From the mid-1990s, St Patrick's Day has been recast as a way to promote Ireland right across the world.

The parades in the main cities, like Cork, Galway, Waterford, Limerick, Kilkenny and Belfast, are now incredible experiences, with millions of visitors arriving to soak up the atmosphere and the high jinks. There are marching bands and majorettes from all over the United States – a nod to the origins of the parade and the fact that we have Irish-Americans to thank for this particular custom.

There are also quieter routes and less extravagant parades, if you prefer a slightly different kind of St Patrick's Day. One popular pilgrimage is to walk up Slemish in County Antrim – about 1,500 people took part in the walk in 2025. In Armagh, as well as music and marching, St Patrick's two cathedrals, one Church of Ireland, the other Catholic, are lit up in vibrant green and there is a candlelit vigil walk from one cathedral to the other to symbolise the unity of the Christian faiths.

And don't forget the local parades. It is an unforgettable experience to go to the cities and be part of a huge crowd of people all out to have fun and see incredible floats and artistry on display. But it is also fantastic to travel out to the towns and villages and see the locals celebrating together. Every square and diamond hosts a parade, usually featuring the local sports clubs, the fire brigade, and local schoolchildren in all manner of costumes and get-ups.

These parades feel wonderfully handmade and homemade and they are all about community. If you find yourself in Drogheda or Donegal town or Ennis or Cobh or Ballyshannon or Westport or Dingle or Killarney or Downpatrick … in any town around the island, do get out and watch the parade. It's what St Patrick's Day started out as and what it's made of at its heart.

## CUSTOMS, OLD AND NEW

### Wearing green

The colour green has a long history in Ireland of representing freedom and sovereignty. It has become absolutely associated with Ireland right across the world. That's why the true hallmark of St Patrick's Day is the ocean of green – from people's clothes, to wigs, to hats, and now even to rivers and buildings as 'greening' becomes a staple part of the festivities. It's a day for county jerseys and a green *geansaí*.

But the key green you are wearing should be a bunch of shamrock. This is usually worn on the lapel, or pinned to your hat. In the St Patrick's Day Masses of days gone by, the whole congregation would be sporting big sprigs of fresh shamrock, often wrapped in a twist of tinfoil to hold it in place for the day. You'll need it if you want to follow another old custom: drowning the shamrock (see below).

*The Wearing of the Green,* print from 1907.

## St Patrick's badges and crosses

This custom has been lost now, but there are surviving examples in the Museum of Country Life in Castlebar, County Mayo, which holds a fascinating and wide-ranging exhibition documenting folklife in Ireland. From the 1600s until the early twentieth century, the day was celebrated by the making of crosses with paper and ribbons. The red cross of St Patrick often featured in these, especially in earlier centuries and among Irish regiments. By the nineteenth century they were only made and worn by children. These were circular badges, made with colourful paper and ribbons, and usually worn on the right shoulder. In the early nineteenth century, silk rosettes could be bought on the streets of Dublin, but after that the custom dwindled away.

## Drowning the shamrock

Lent is a period of abstinence, from Ash Wednesday until Easter Sunday, which means alcohol and meat are off the menu. But thanks to St Patrick, there is one day when the rules can be broken without consequence. This has led to the day being firmly associated with partaking of a Guinness or several. There is an old custom that is not so much in practice now of turning the final nightcap into a bit of good luck. When drinking the last whiskey, the custom was to remove your shamrock from your lapel and drop it into the glass to 'drown' it and toast St Patrick. The whiskey was drunk, whereupon the shamrock was thrown over the left shoulder for luck.

## St Patrick's fishes

This old custom has fallen by the wayside, but it provides an insight into how to fashion a handy loophole. Lent was a very strict affair in twentieth-century Ireland – no meat, dairy or eggs, no drinking, dancing or weddings. In a good example of giving an inch and taking a mile, a folk story was told about Patrick eating meat during Lent, much to his shame. An angel appeared and told him to take his meat to the spring and dip it in the water. Patrick did so, and the meat miraculously changed into fish – which meant Patrick had consumed fish, not meat, and therefore broken no holy laws. By the same gesture, Irish people could dip their meat in water, and thereby consume 'fish' on St Patrick's Day.

## Atin' and drinkin'

There might not be too many Irish households left that prepare a special meal on St Patrick's Day, but the pubs will certainly serve you the traditional bacon and cabbage. In Dublin, coddle is another favourite, and the traditional boxty and champ will usually be offered as well. There used to be houses where a green, white and orange meal would be served, such as ham with potato, cabbage and carrots. The other traditional and delicious dishes are stew and soda bread. The traditional drinks haven't changed for a couple of centuries: Guinness and whiskey.

## Did you know?

✤ The title of smallest parade in Ireland – and indeed the world – was held in the twentieth century by the village of Dripsey in County Cork. The villagers paraded 25 yards/23m from The Lee Valley Inn to The Weigh Inn – out one pub door and in the other. In the twenty-first century, the crown has been taken by Curragraigue in County Wexford. Started in 2018, it features the locals parading around The Commons. There are no spectators here – everyone is in the parade. Talking about the 2025 parade, organiser Michael Fortune said: *'As usual, we don't have a plan as such but more than likely there will be a St. Patrick, possibly a traditional music marching band, always a few stray dogs, a vintage tractor ... maybe an American and always a few cold-looking children.'* So if you like the idea of being in the smallest parade in Ireland, just turn up at Curragraigue in your walking shoes on 17 March!

A nineteenth-century *cailín,* (Irish for 'girl' or 'young woman'). Each year a young woman was chosen to represent festivities in some communities on St Patrick's Day.

## CHAPTER 12:
# The Greening of the World – St Patrick's Day Beyond Ireland

*Whether we are Irish by birth or Irish by choice, we are all part of a rich and vibrant global community that is bound together by a shared love of life, a shared love of our national heritage, language and culture.*

Former president of Ireland,
Michael D. Higgins, St Patrick's
Day Message 2023

Former president
Michael D. Higgins
in Galway.